St. George Ontario Book 1 in Colour Photos, Saving Our History One Photo at a Time

Photography
by Barbara Raué
2017

Series Name:
Cruising Ontario

Book 180: St. George Book 1

Cover photo: 18 Beverly Street East, Page 50

Series Name: Cruising Ontario
Saving Our History One Photo at a Time
in colour photos

Books Available in Alphabetical Order:
Aberfoyle, Acton, Alton, Amherstburg, Ancaster, Arthur, Aylmer, Ayr, Bloomingdale, Brantford, Burlington, Caledon, Caledonia, Cambridge, Clifford, Conestogo, Delhi, Dorchester to Aylmer, Drayton, Drumbo, Dundas, Eden Mills, Elmira, Elora, Essex, Fergus, Guelph, Hagersville, Hamilton, Hanover, Harriston, Hespeler, Jarvis, Kingston, Kingsville, Kitchener, Linwood, Listowel, London, Lucknow, Mono, Mount Forest, Neustadt, New Hamburg, Niagara-on-the-Lake, Oakville, Orangeville, Orillia, Owen Sound, Palmerston, Peterborough, Petrolia, Port Elgin, Preston, Rockwood, Sarnia, Seaforth, Sheffield, Shelburne, Simcoe, Southampton, St. Jacobs, St. Marys, St. Thomas, Stoney Creek, Stratford, Thamesford, Tillsonburg, Waterdown, Waterford, Waterloo, Welland, Wellesley, Windsor, Wingham, Woodstock

Book 146-149: Ottawa
Book 156: Morrisburg
Book 157: Brockville
Book 158: Merrickville
Book 159: Smiths Falls
Book 160: Portland, Newboro
Book 161: Westport & Area
Book 162: Perth
Book 163-166: Belleville
Book 167-168: Port Colborne
Book 169: Erin in Colour
Book 170: Goderich in Colour
Book 171: Sault Ste. Marie
Book 172: Lake Superior

Book 173-176: Thunder Bay
Book 177-179: Paris
Book 180-181: St. George
Book 182-183: Burford
Book 184: Mt Pleasant, Onondaga, Newport

Other Books by Barbara Raue

Coins of Gold

Arrows, Indians and Love

The Life and Times of Barbara
Volume 1: Inventions That Have Enhanced My Life
Volume 2: Entertainment That I Have Enjoyed
Volume 3: East Coast Trips
Volume 4: Olympics Have Always Intrigued Me
Volume 5: Wonders of the World
Volume 6: Caribbean Cruises We Have Enjoyed
Volume 7: Animals
Volume 8: Storms and Other Major Disasters in My Lifetime
Volume 9: Wars, Terrorist Attacks and Major Disasters

The Cromwell Family Book

Laura Secord Discovered

Daddy Where Are You?

Montana Series
Book 1: Montana Dream
Book 2: Life on the Montana Frontier
Book 3: Montana to Boston and Back
Book 4: Montana Sons Go to War
Book 5: Montana Sons Return From War

Visit Barbara's website to view all of her books
http://barbararaue.ca

Table of Contents

Thompson Street	Page 6
West Street	Page 7
Beverly Street West	Page 11
Main Street South	Page 17
Main Street North	Page 29
High Street	Page 37
Tolhurst Avenue	Page 41
Beverly Street East	Page 48
Architectural Terms	Page 62
Building Styles	Page 67

The County of Brant is located at the mid-point of the Grand River as it flows south from Luther Marsh to Lake Erie. In Brant, the river flows through an area of rich farmland and Carolinian forest. The river was used for water power and transportation. European settlers first arrived in Burford Township in 1793 and began to settle in the rest of the County soon after.

In 1852 the City of Brantford, the Village of Paris, and the Townships of Brantford, Oakland, Onondaga, South Dumfries, and Burford became Brant County.

Two hundred years ago, Obed Wilson ventured forth seeking an area in Upper Canada in which to settle. He discovered a place with fertile land, sparkling water and natural beauty which enticed him to stay and build a log cabin. Eventually the vision grew into the Village of St. George.

St. George, located to the north of the City of Brantford, is in the Township of South Dumfries. It was founded in 1814. John and Peter Bauslaugh were early settlers in St. George, and the early name of the village was "Bauslaugh Mills" in honour of John Bauslaugh who owned a sawmill near Highway 99. Main Street began to develop in the 1820s when Henry Moe began selling fish and dry goods from the first log building. By 1832, the village had three churches and several businesses. Today Main Street continues to thrive with many of the original buildings from the 1800s attracting people to the antique shops, cafes and restaurants.

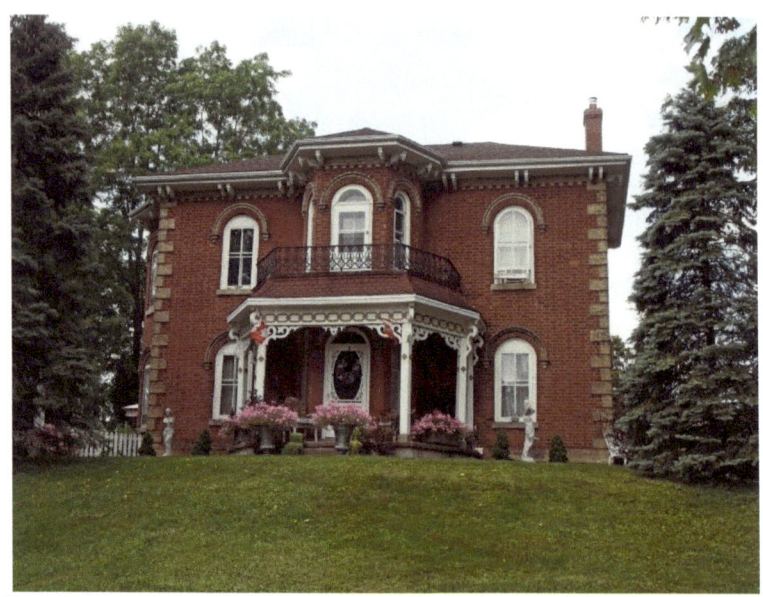

6 Thompson Street – Two Roses Bed & Breakfast – Italianate – bay window with balcony, corner quoins

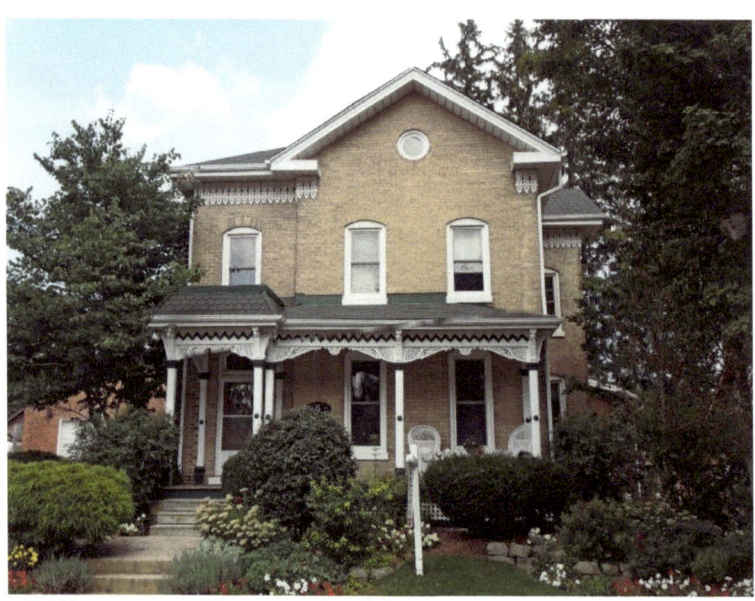

5 Thompson Street – Gothic, cornice return on gable

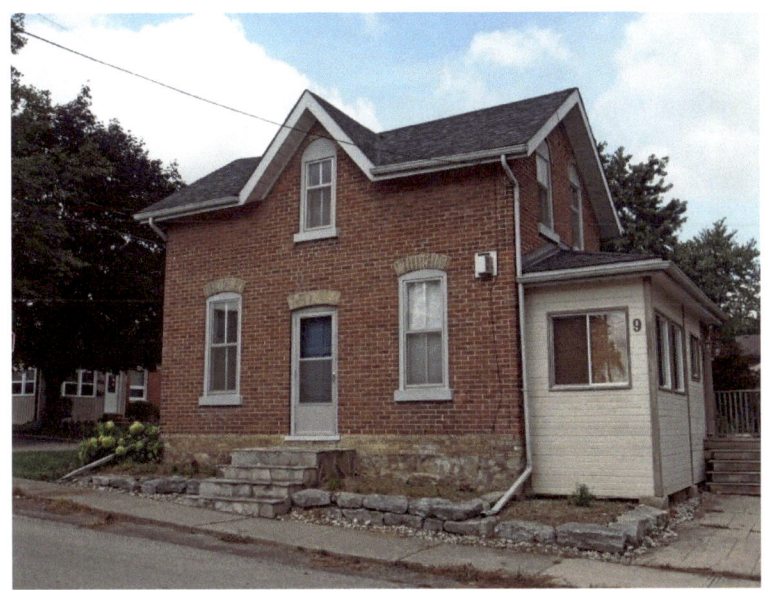

9 Thompson Street – Gothic

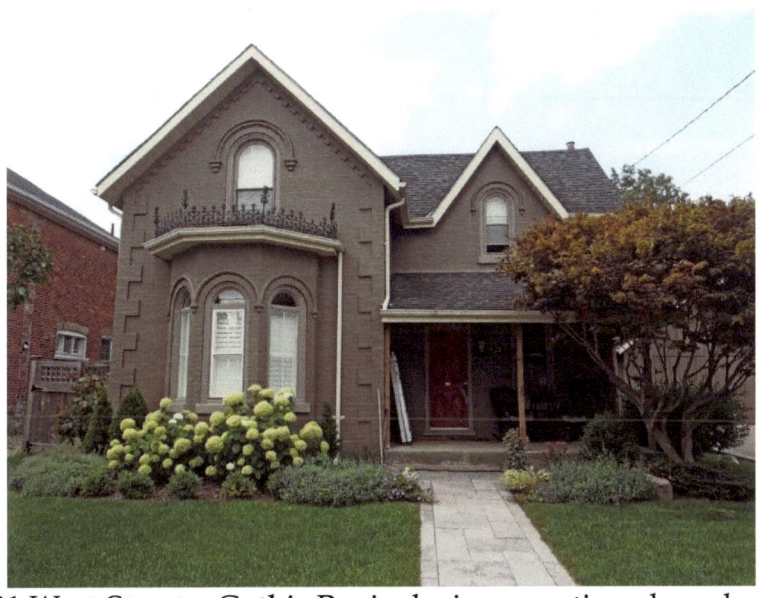

21 West Street – Gothic Revival – iron cresting above bay window

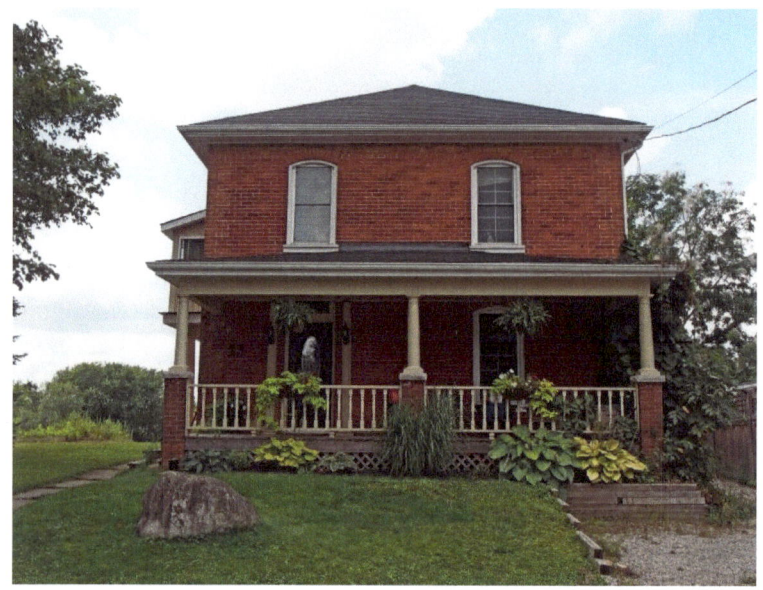

23 West Street – hipped roof

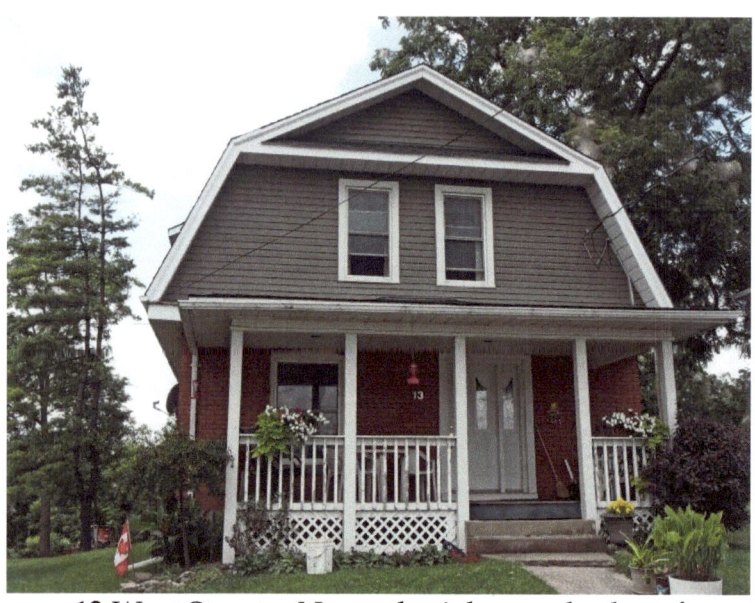

13 West Street – Neo-colonial – gambrel roof

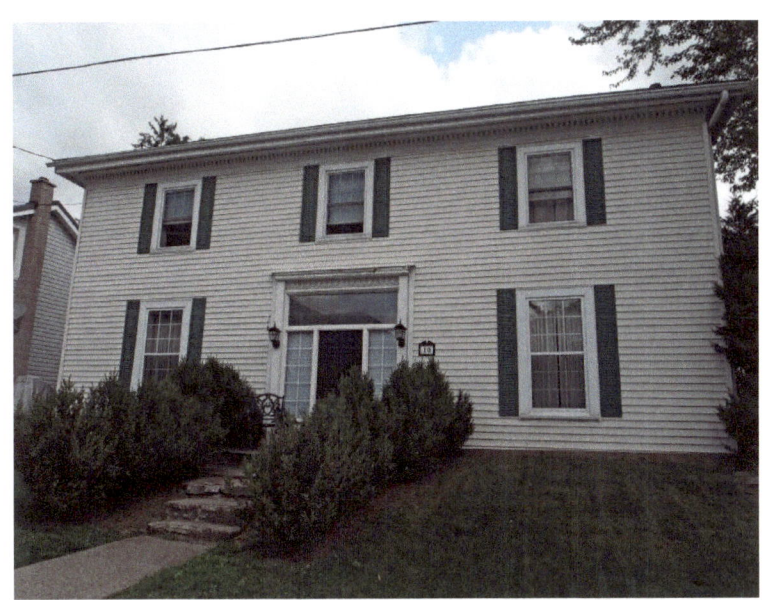

10 West Street - Georgian

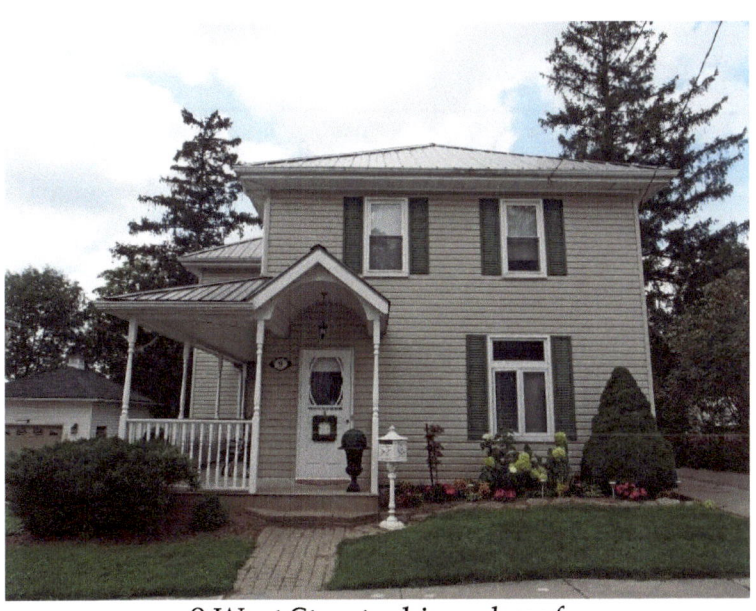

9 West Street – hipped roof

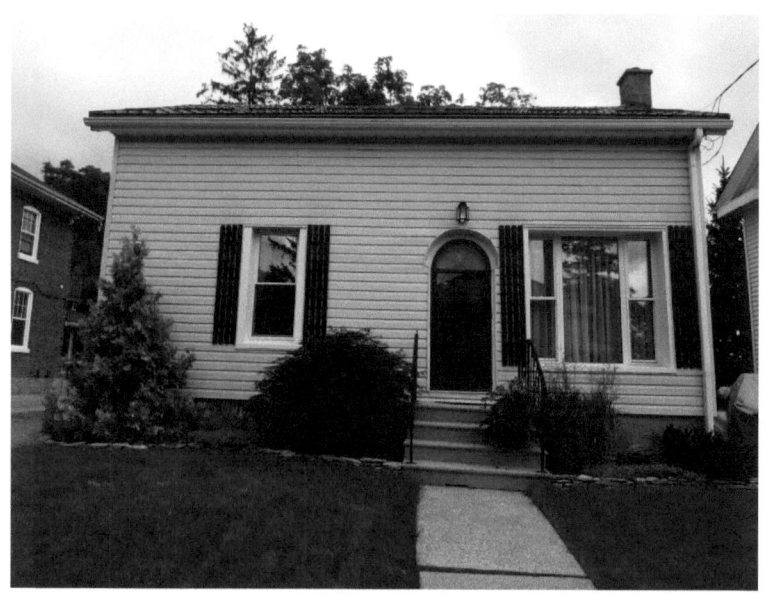

8 West Street

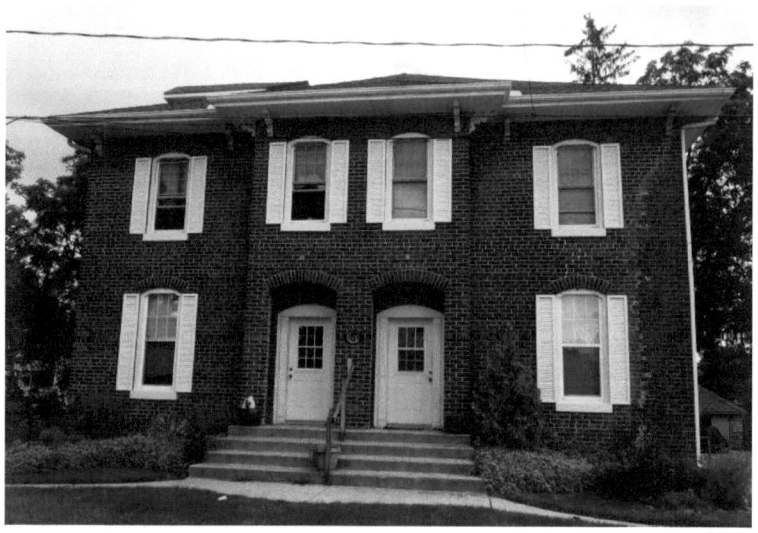

4 & 6 West Street

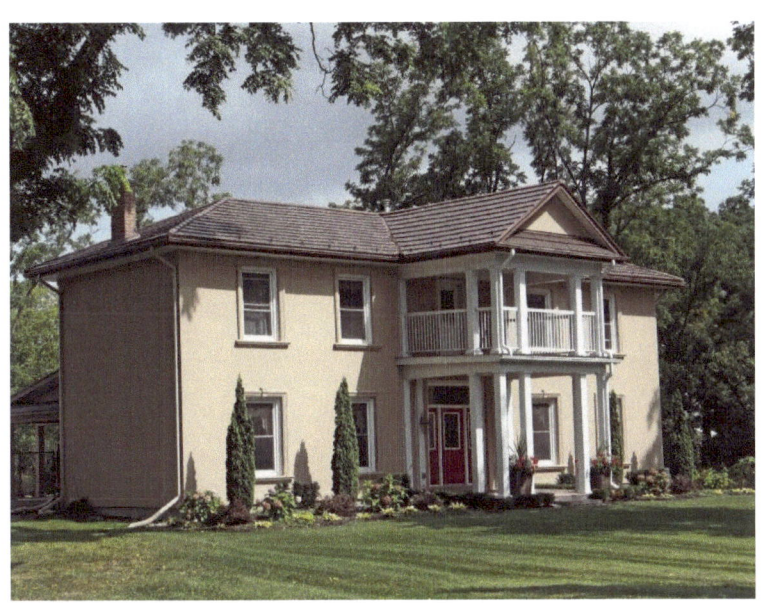

209 Beverly Street West

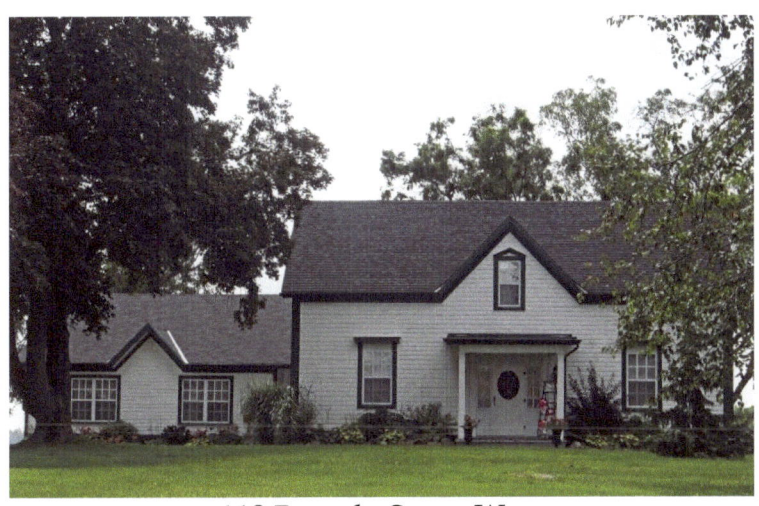

110 Beverly Street West

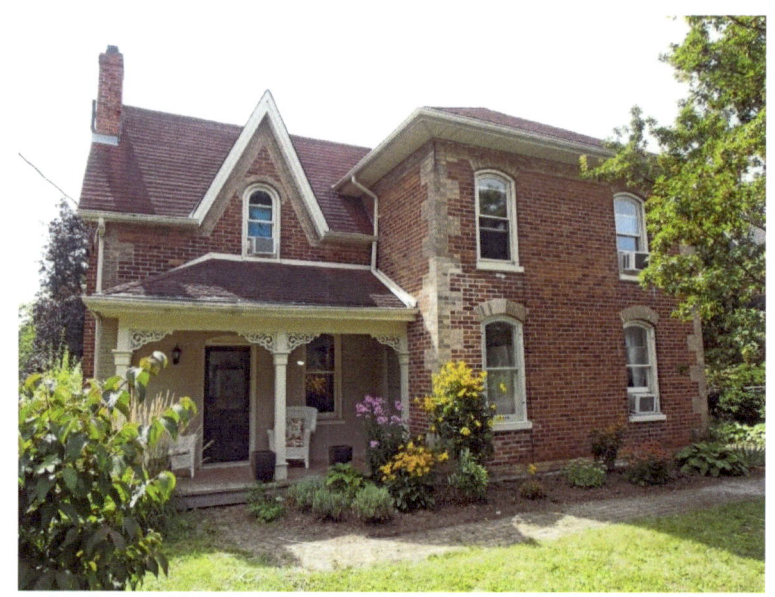

Beverly Street West – Gothic – dichromatic brickwork, corner quoins, voussoirs

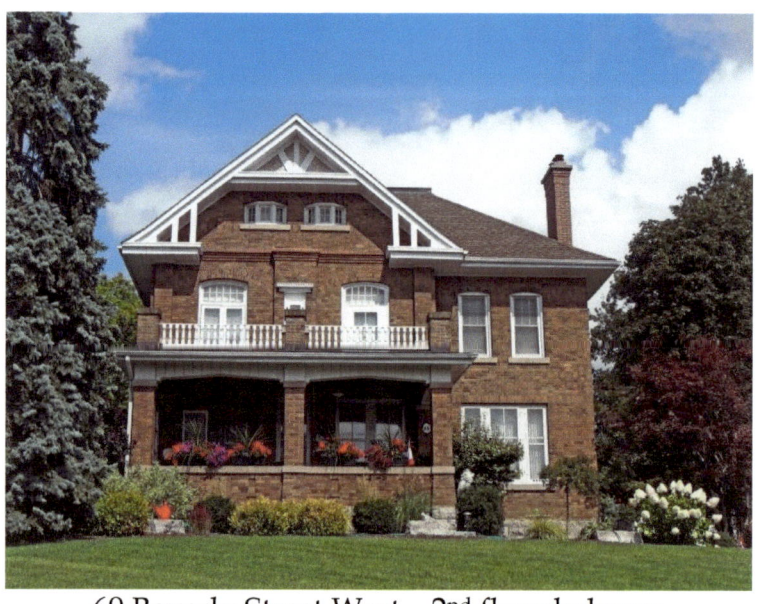

69 Beverly Street West – 2nd floor balcony

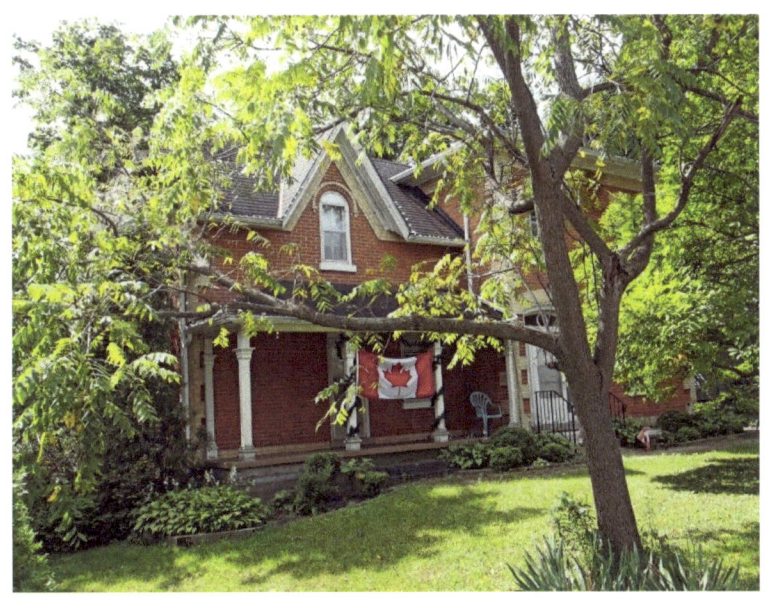

68 Beverly Street West – Gothic, corner quoins

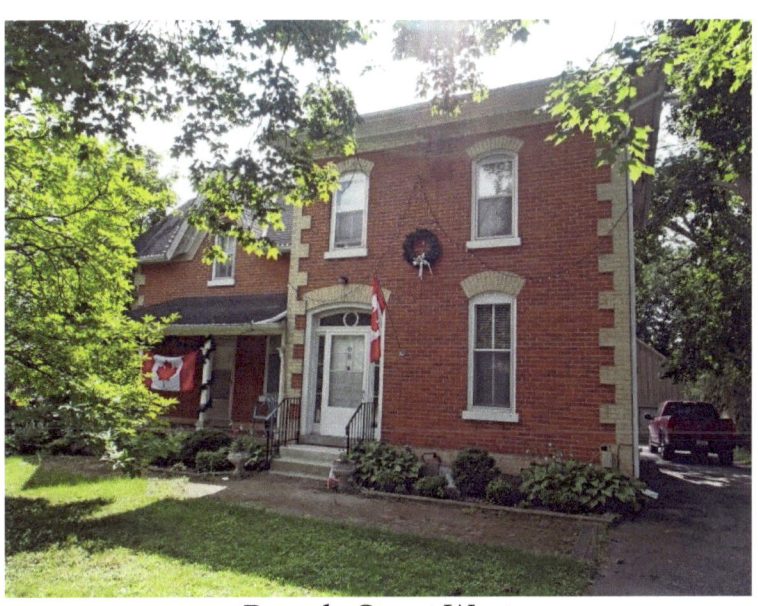

Beverly Street West

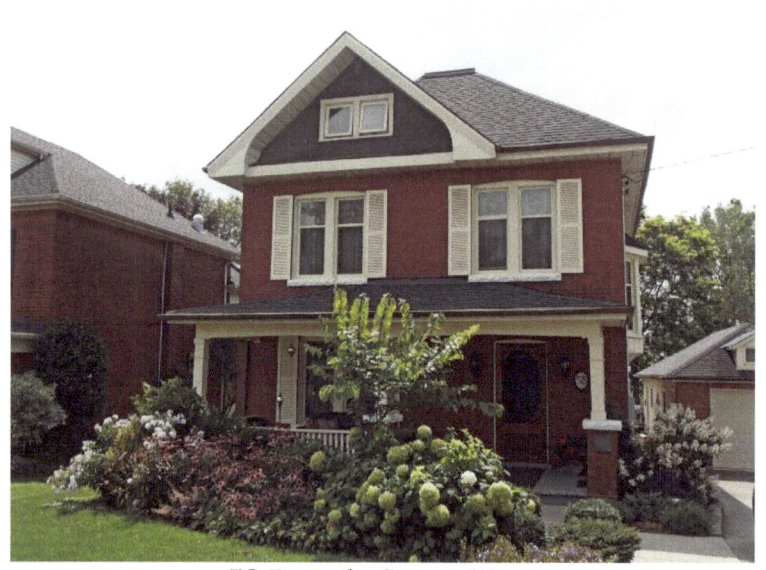

58 Beverly Street West

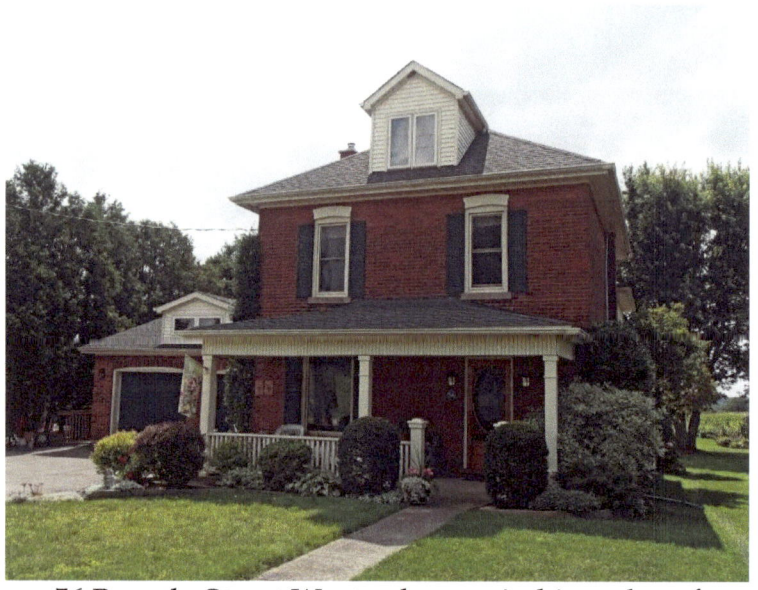

56 Beverly Street West – dormer in hipped roof

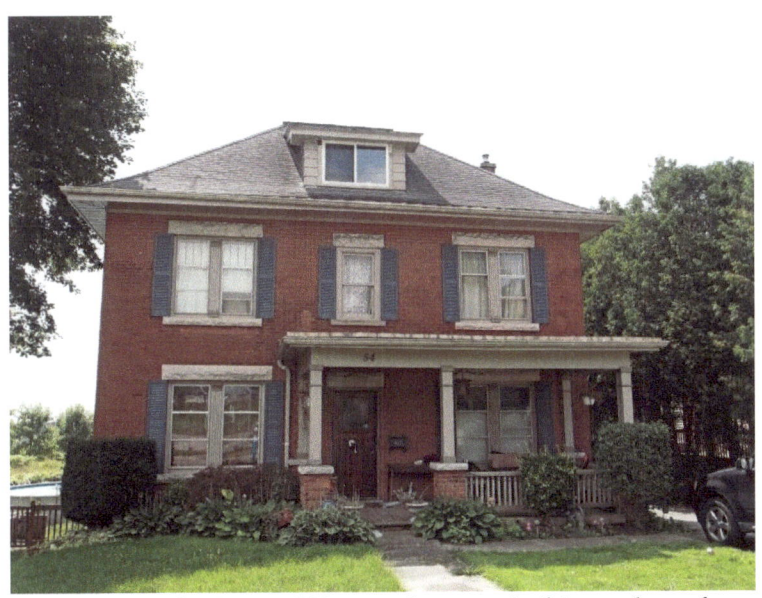

54 Beverly Street West – dormer in hipped roof

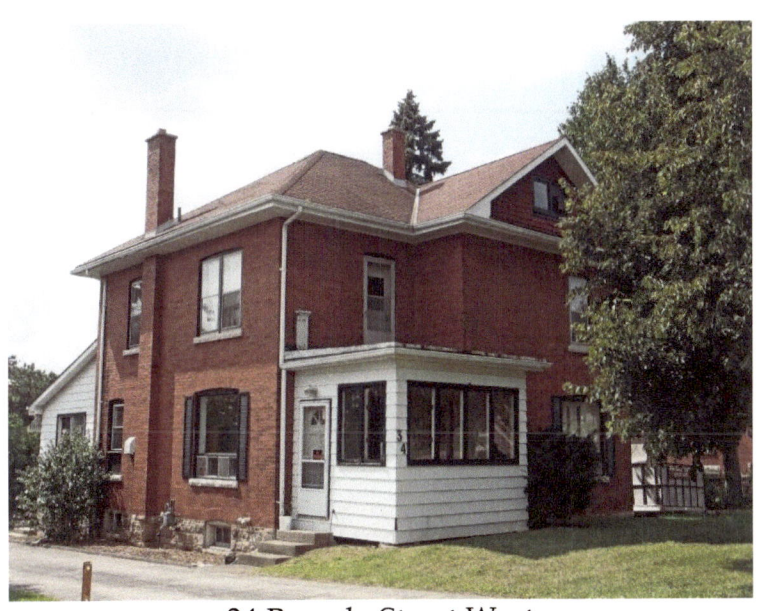

34 Beverly Street West

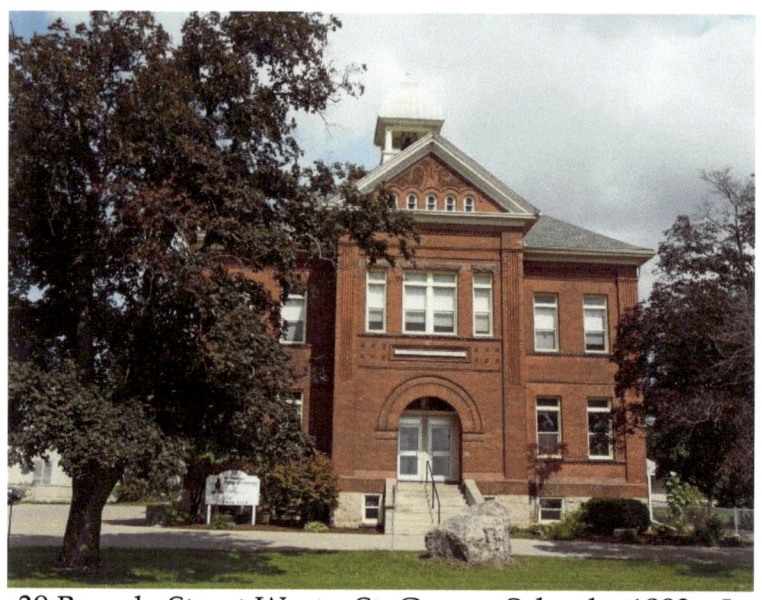

39 Beverly Street West – St. George School – 1893 – It remained in use as a school until another one was built behind it in 1973. Today, a children's nursery school and day care centre operate here.

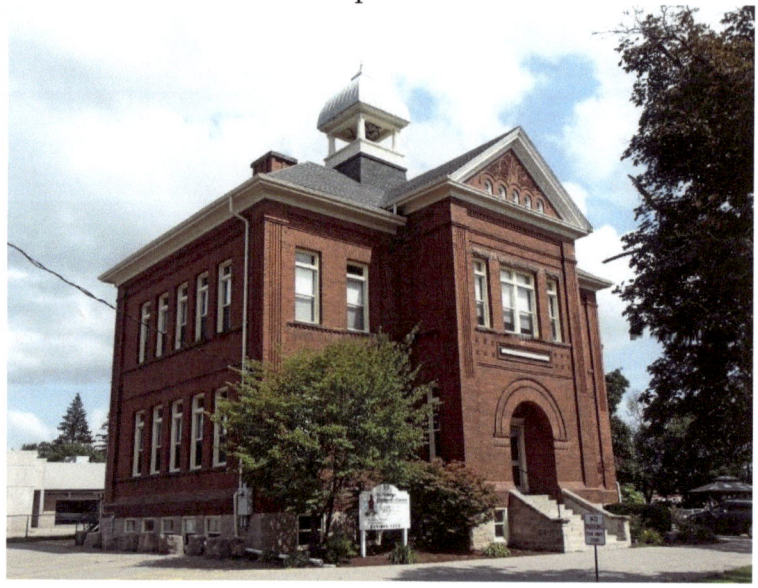

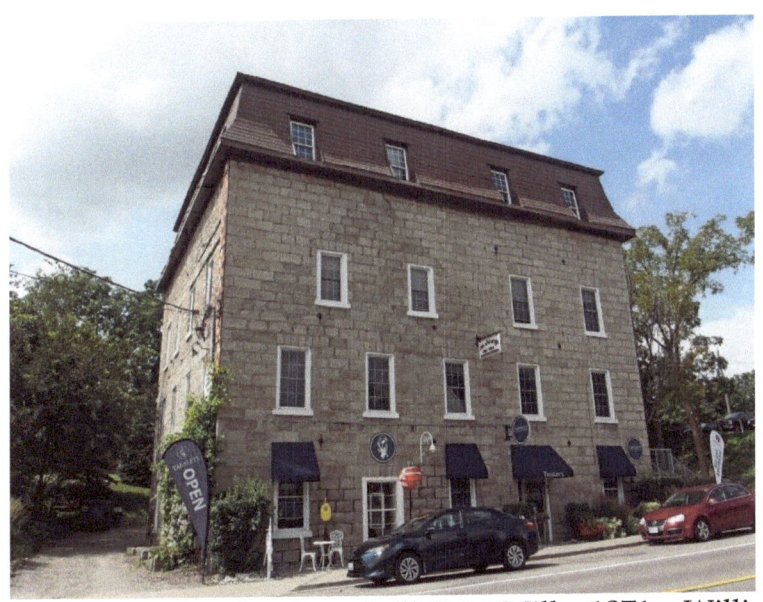

41 Main Street South – Snowball Grist Mill – 1871 – William Snowball began construction of this cut and dressed stone flour mill in 1869. In the summer of 1885, steam power was added and alterations were made that enabled the mill to turn out two hundred barrels of flour per day. It operated as St. George Feed & Seed Mill from 1967 to 1993.

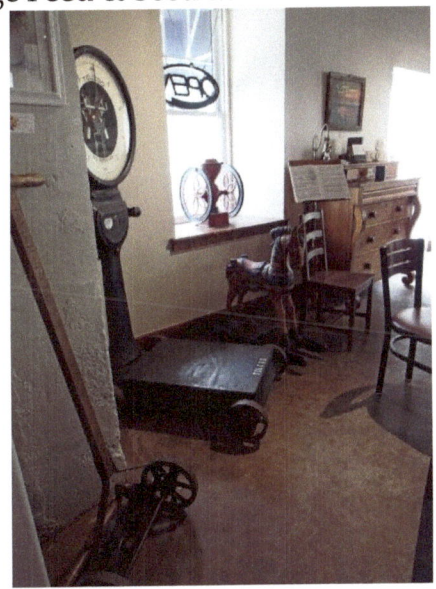

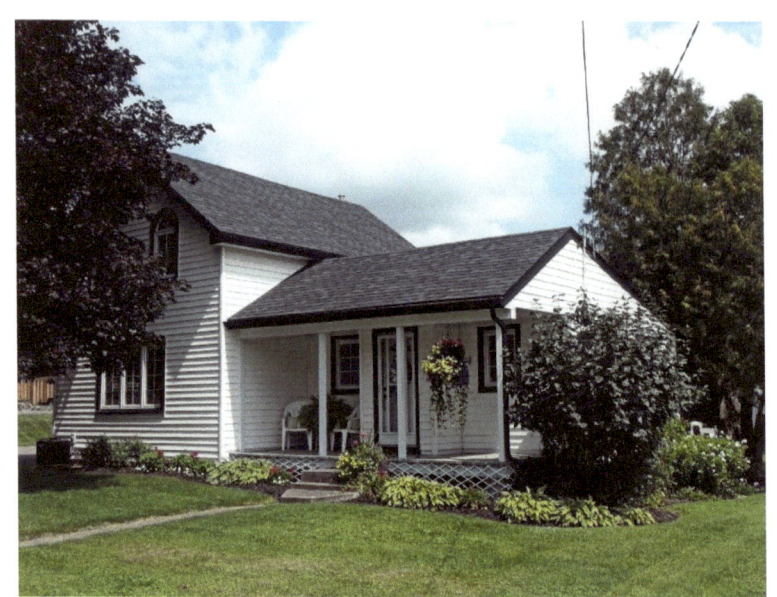

Main Street South

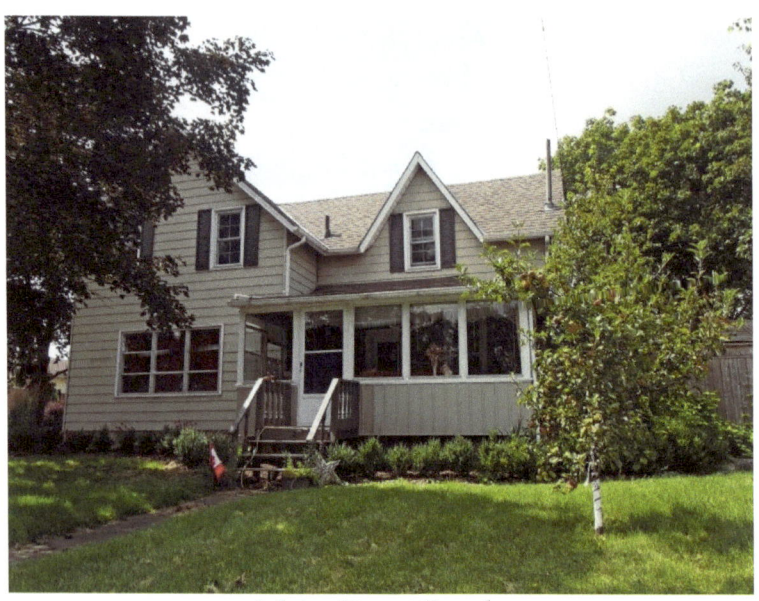

Main Street South

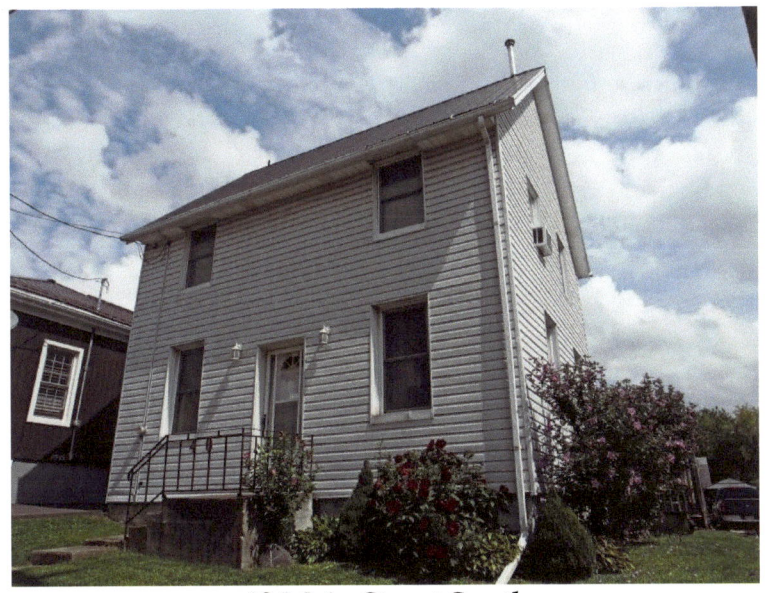

40 Main Street South

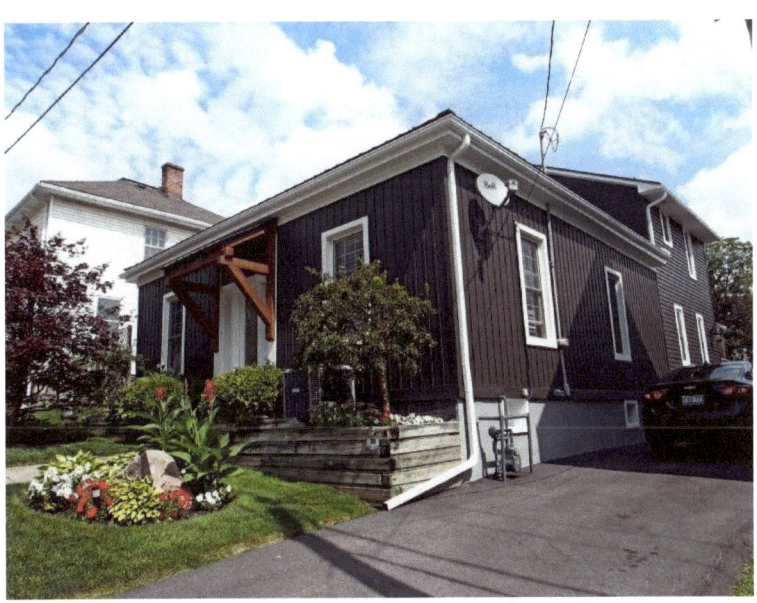

38 Main Street South

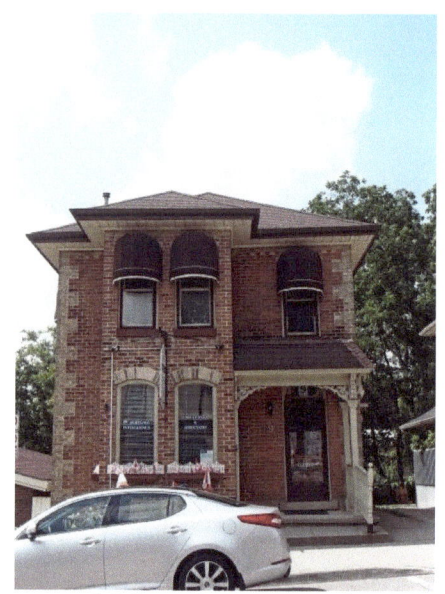

9 Main Street South

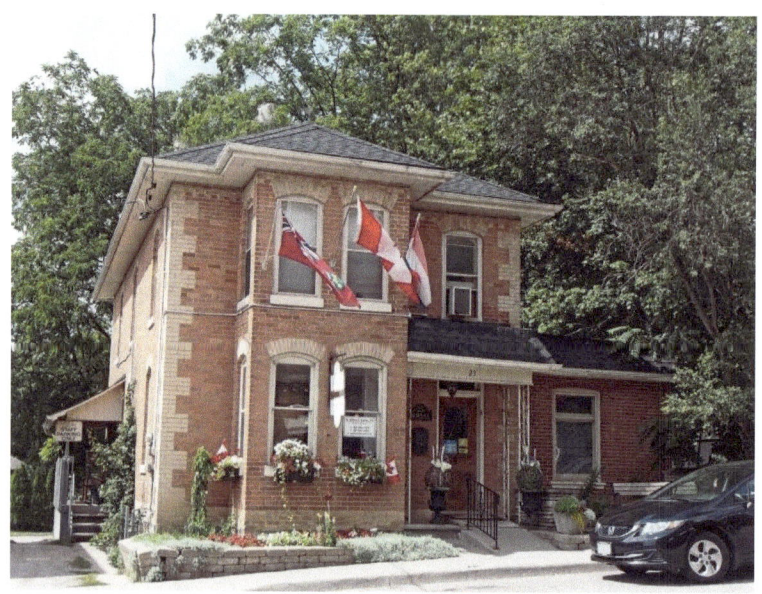

23 Main Street South

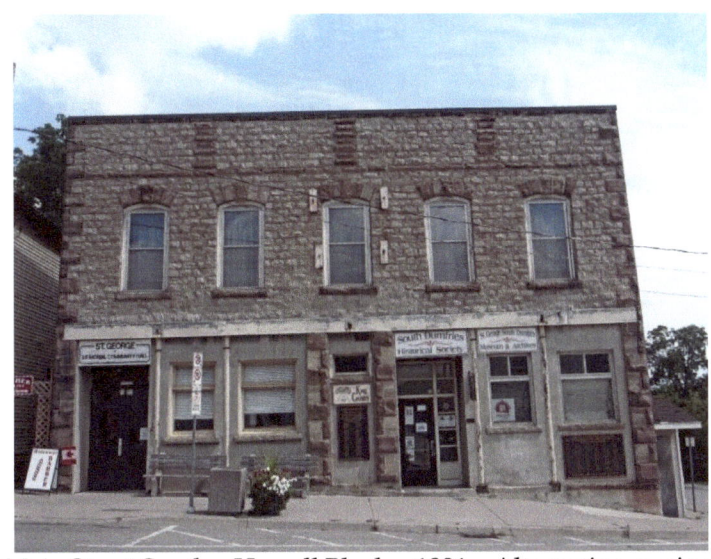

34-36 Main Street South – Howell Block – 1891 – Alternating quoins on the corners of the building and ornamental arches with center keystones over the windows are of contrasting color. Since 1924, the stone building has housed the post office, library and space for community groups. Now it is the home of the South Dumfries Historical Society.

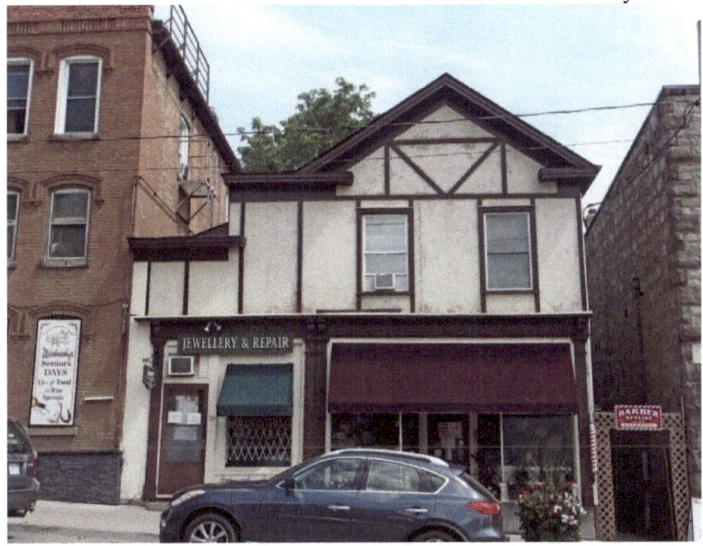

30 Main Street South – Savory Goldsmithing - The Reid Block is a stone building constructed in 1875 by David Reid Sr. who set up his furniture and undertaking shop.

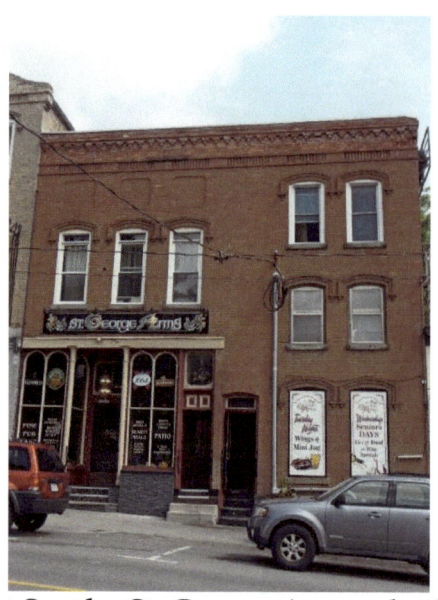

24 Main Street South - St. George Arms, also known as the Richardson Block, was built of red brick and completed in 1887.

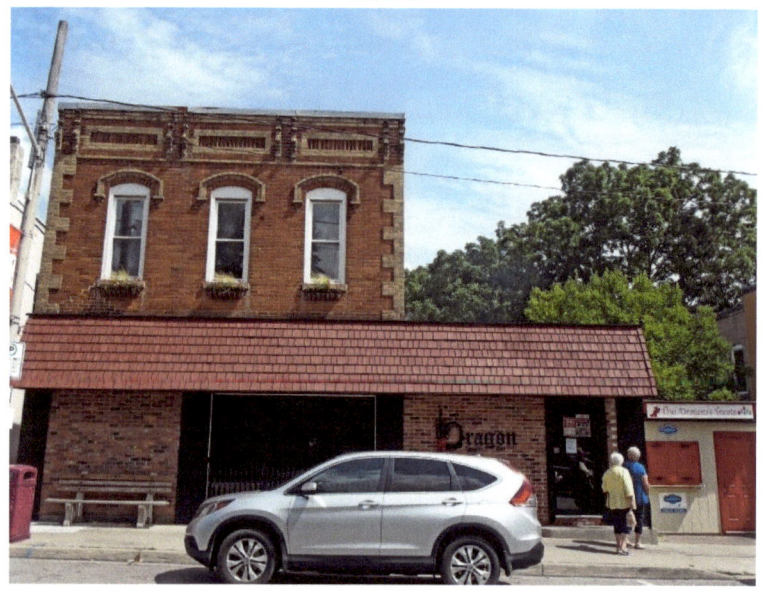

14 Main Street South – the Dragon Sports Bar

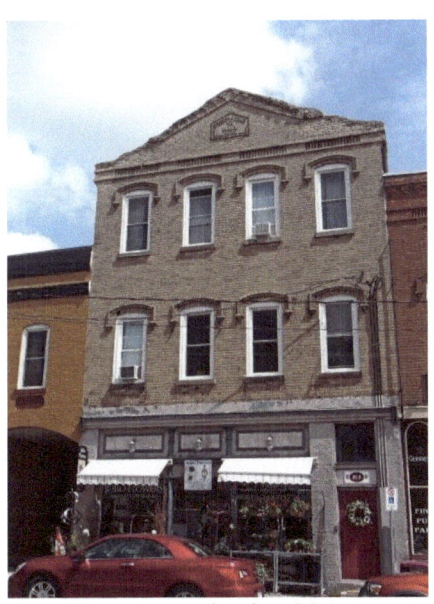

20 Main Street South - Haas Block 1886, Free Masons Hall on the third floor

Freemasonry, the oldest fraternal organization in the world, is dedicated to the Brotherhood of Man under the Fatherhood of God. Freemasonry welcomes into its midst men of any race or religious belief, as long as they profess a belief in one supreme being. It is not a religion, but does encourage its members to be faithful to their own particular beliefs. It is an organization dedicated to personal betterment through education of the inner self. It encourages its members to place high value on morality and virtue.

My Brother, Masonry means much more
Than the wearing of a pin,
Or carrying a paid-up dues receipt
So the Lodge will let you in.

You may wear an emblem on your coat,
From your finger flash a ring,
But if you're not sincere at heart
This doesn't mean a thing.

It's merely an outward sign to show
The world that you belong
To this great fraternal brotherhood
That teaches right from wrong.

What really counts lies buried deep
Within the human breast,
'Til Masonic teaching brings it out
And puts it to the test.

If you practice out of Lodge
The things you learn within,
Be just and upright to yourself
And to your fellowmen.

Console a brother when he's sick
And assist him when in need,
Without a thought of personal reward
For any act or deed.

Walk and act in such a way
That the world without can see
That only the best can meet the test
Laid down by Masonry.

Be always faithful to your trust
And do the best you can
Then you can proudly tell the world
You're a Mason and a Man.

Author unknown

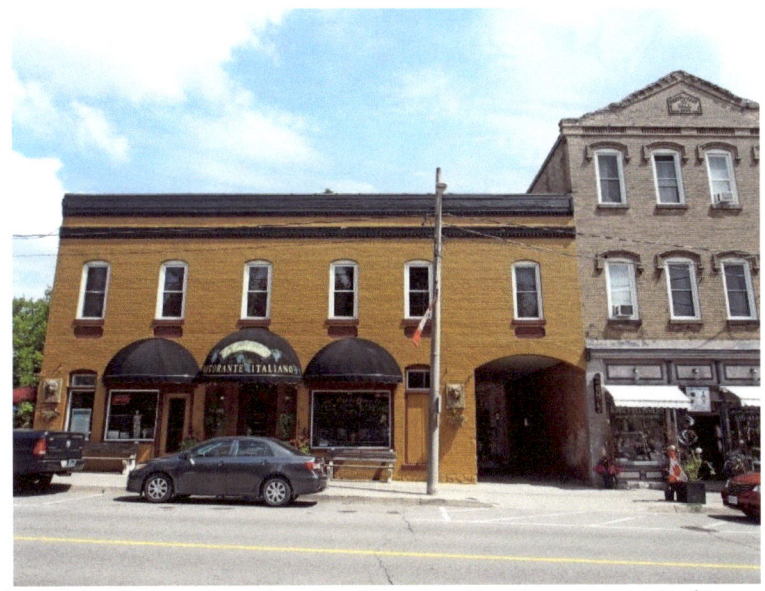

16 Main Street South – La Cantinella Ristorante Italiano - Cummings and Beemer built it in Italianate style in 1886. The original coach entrance to the livery stable which was behind the hotel is still there.

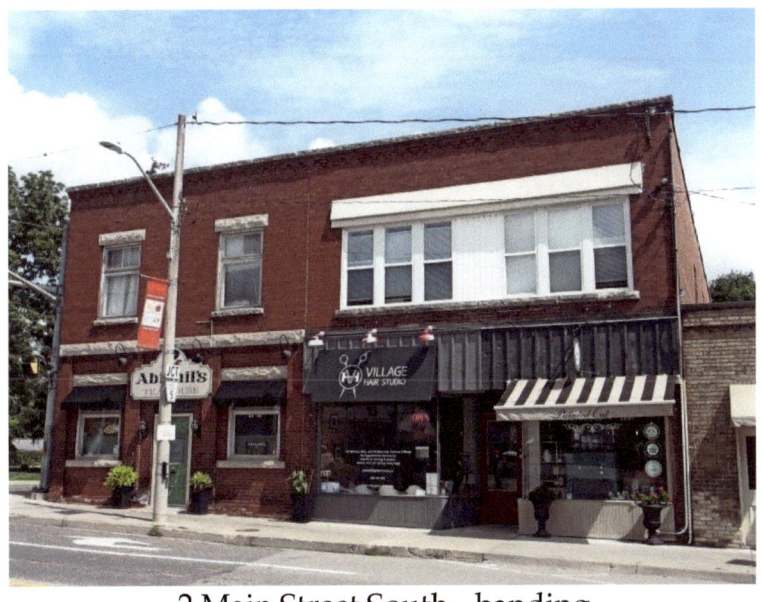

2 Main Street South - banding

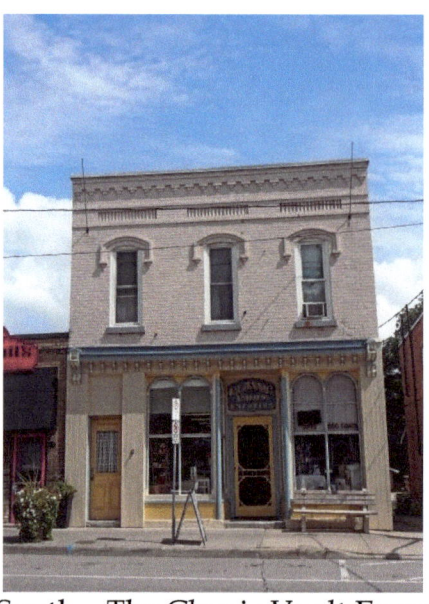

12 Main Street South – The Classic Vault Emporium After the fire in August1887, Robert Hickox removed the rubble and built his famous two-storey store where he sold stoves and hardware and had his tin ware business. If you couldn't find what you were looking for here, it hadn't been made yet.

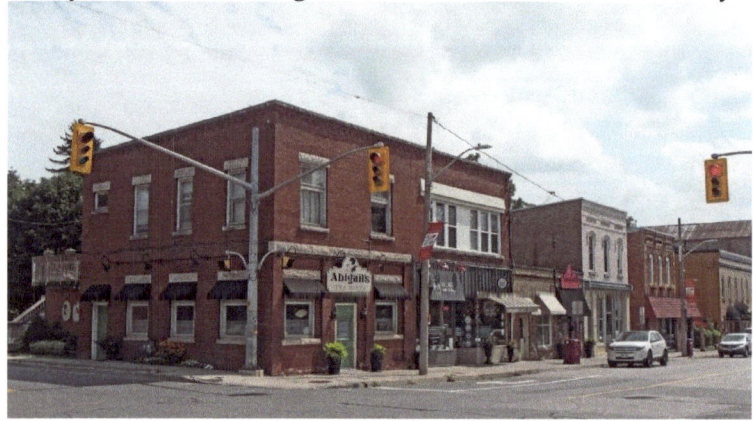

Built in 1911 - It was first occupied by the Merchants Bank of Canada which later merged with the Bank of Montreal. Banks like to locate their buildings on corners as it symbolizes strength.

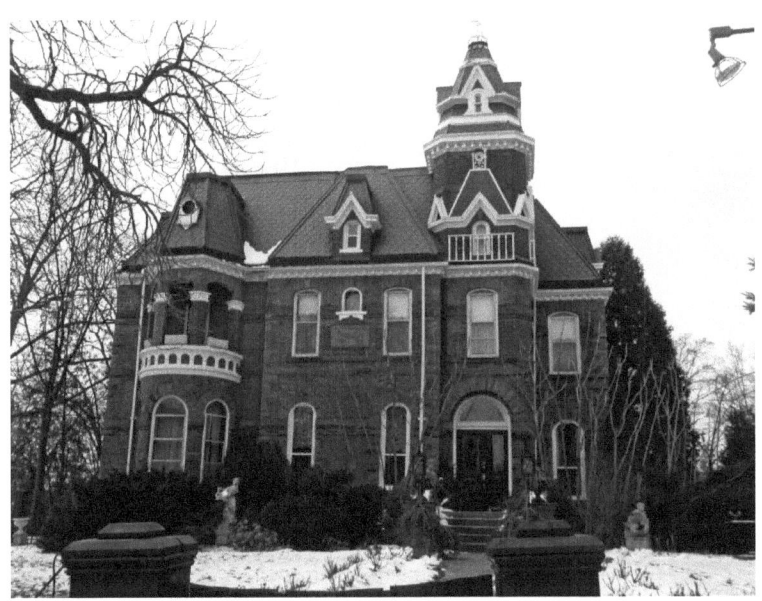

13 Main Street South – Sunnyside – c. 1888 – was constructed by Dr. E.E. Kitchen. It was the heartbeat of Main Street. It was the home of the inaugural meeting of the St. George Women's Institute, January 13, 1903.

This Romanesque Revival mansion was built as a residence and doctor's office. On the third floor there was a ballroom.

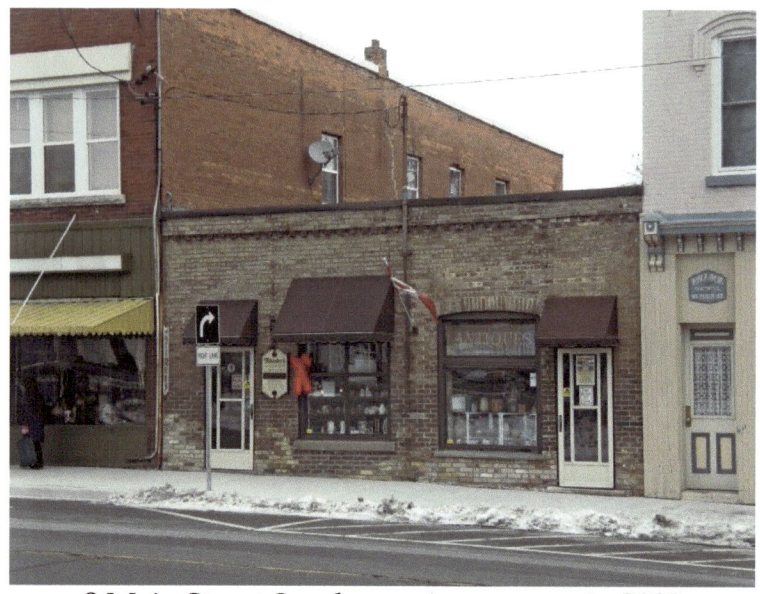
8 Main Street South – antiques store in 2008

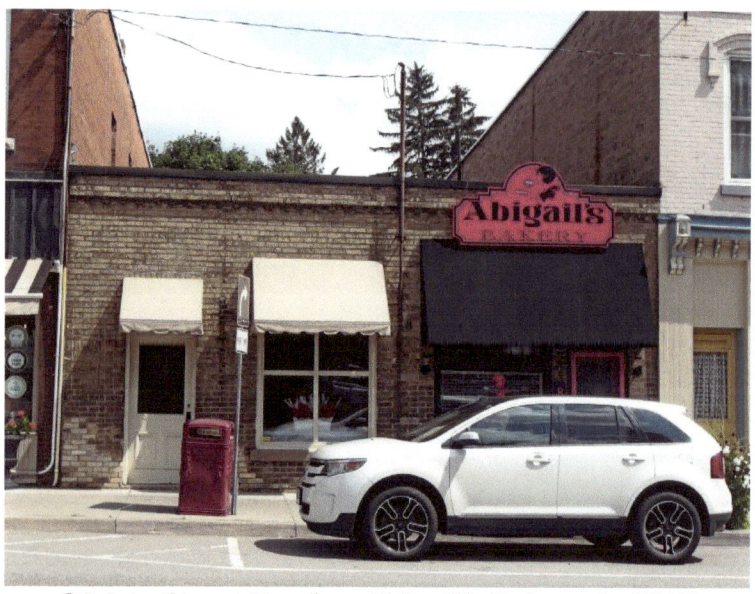
8 Main Street South – Abigail's Bakery in 2017

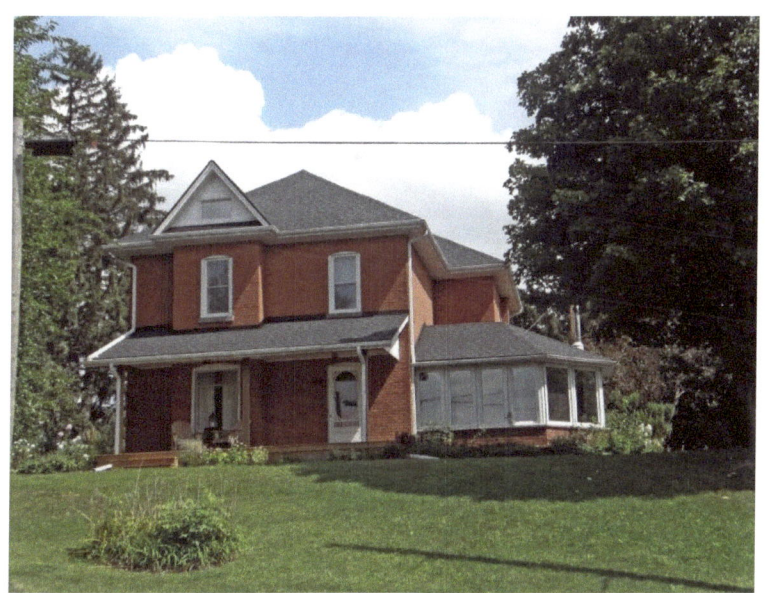

44 Main Street North

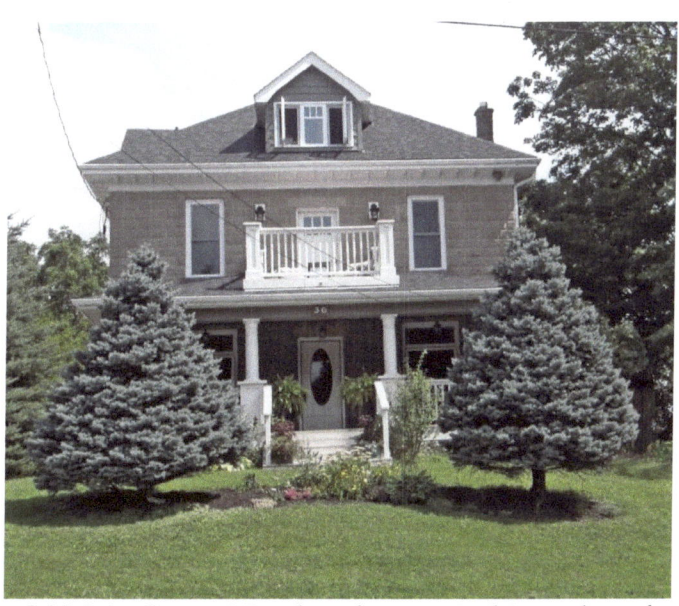

36 Main Street North – dormer in hipped roof

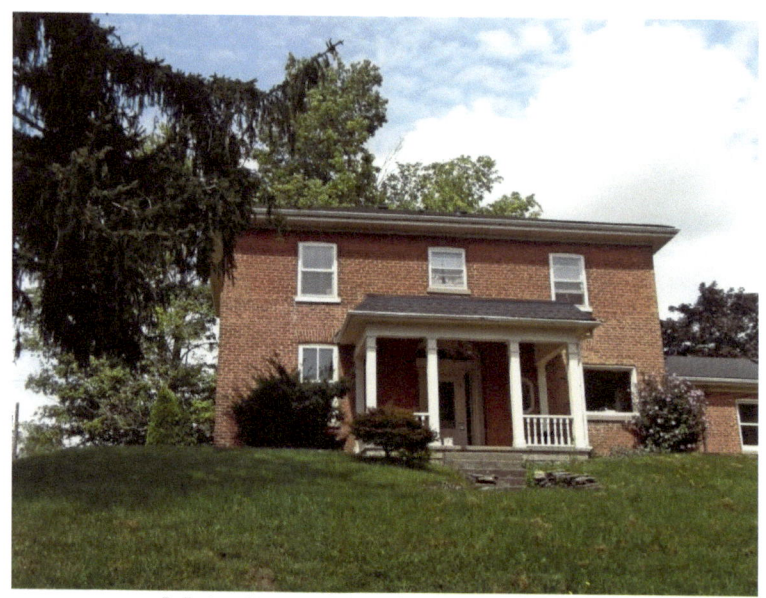
Main Street North – hipped roof

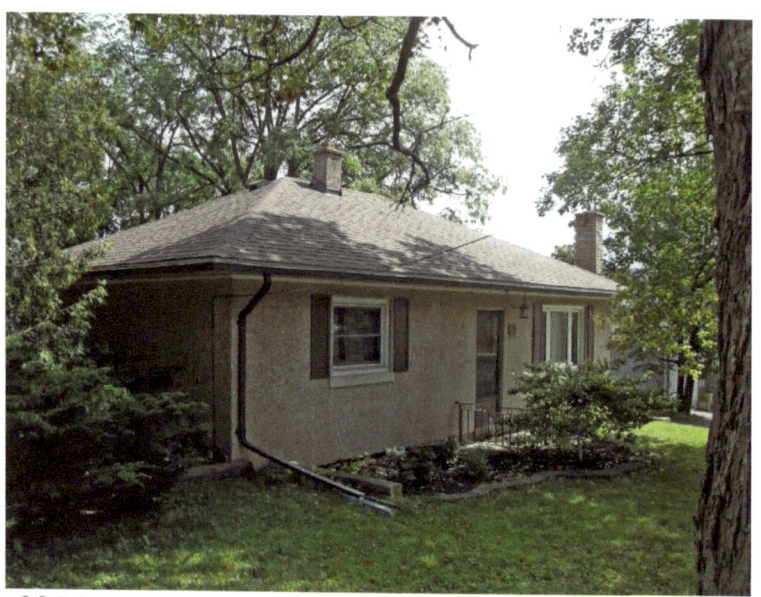
30 Main Street North – Ontario Cottage, hipped roof

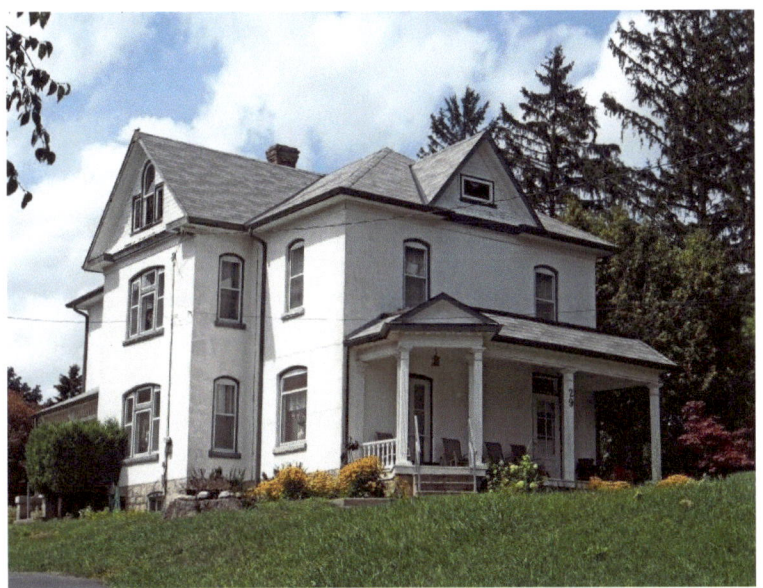

29 Main Street North – Palladian window in two-and-a-half-storey frontispiece on the side, pediment above verandah

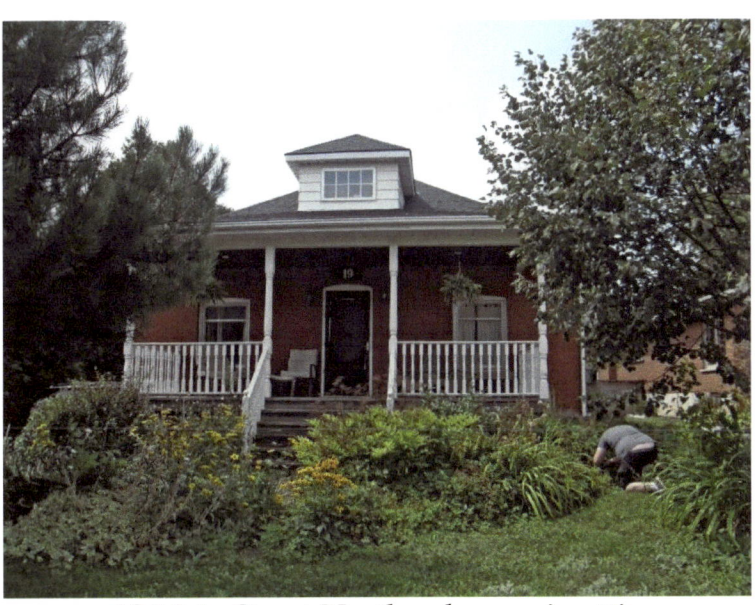

19 Main Street North – dormer in attic

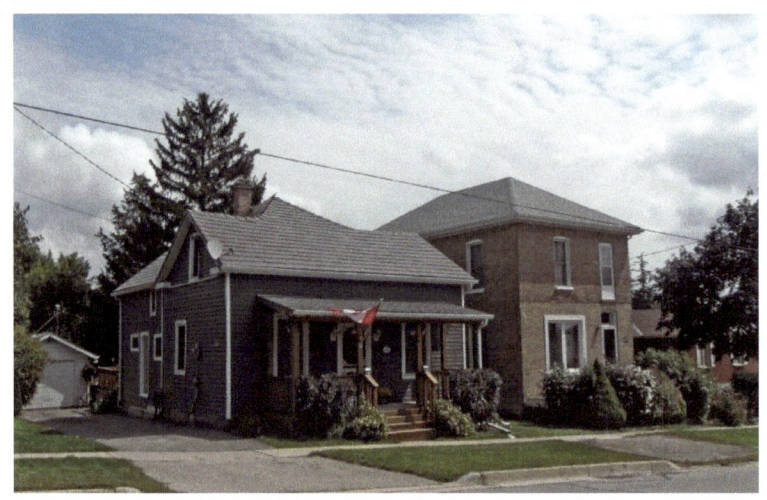

24 and 22 Main Street North

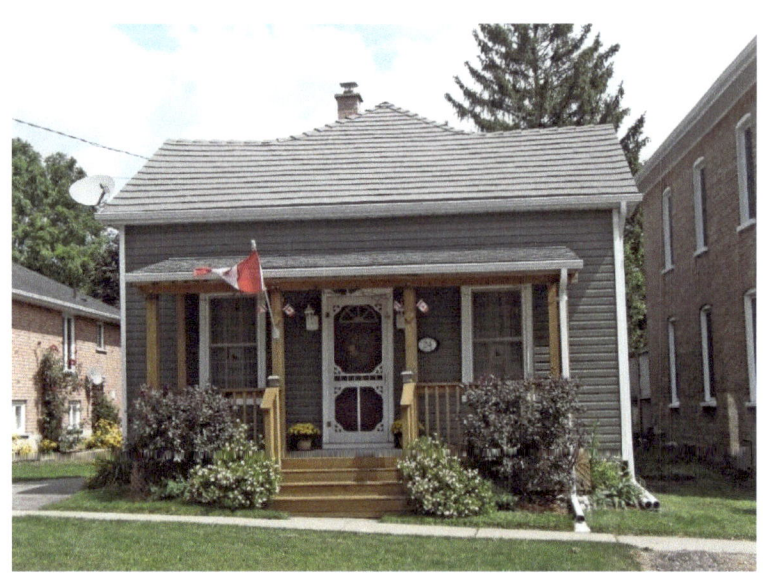

24 Main Street North

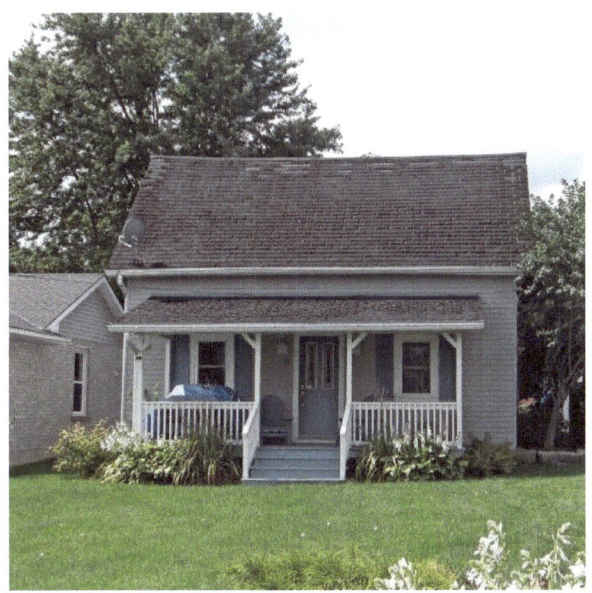

17 Main Street North

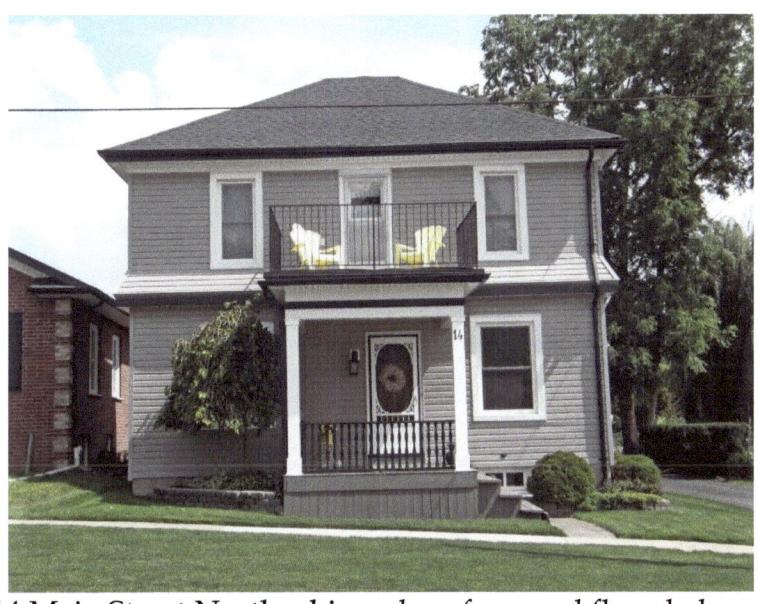

14 Main Street North – hipped roof, second floor balcony

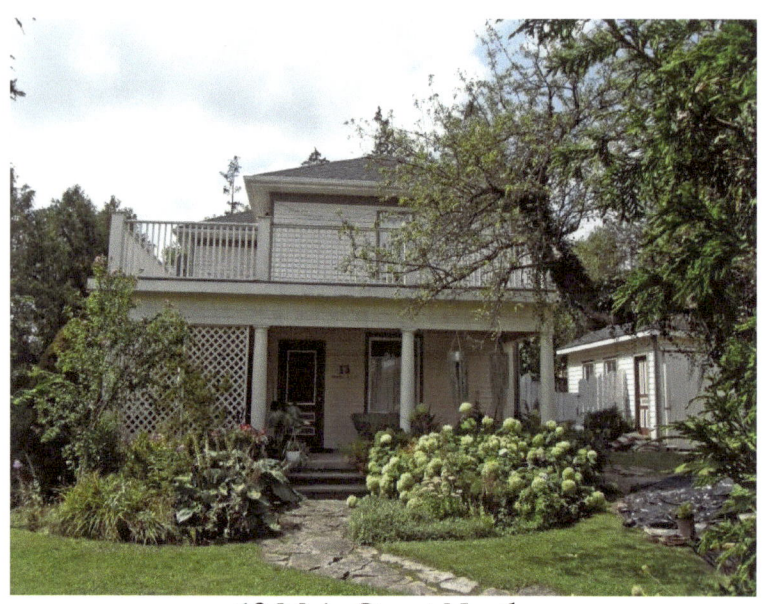

13 Main Street North

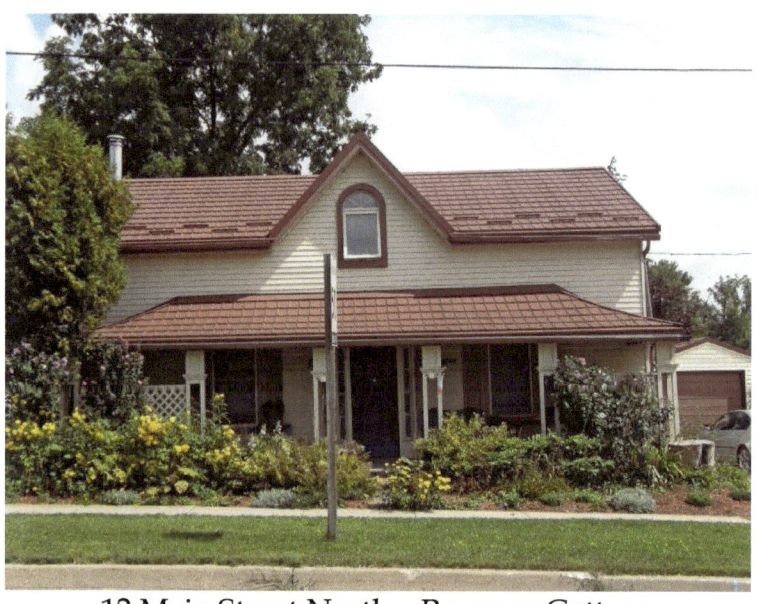

12 Main Street North – Regency Cottage

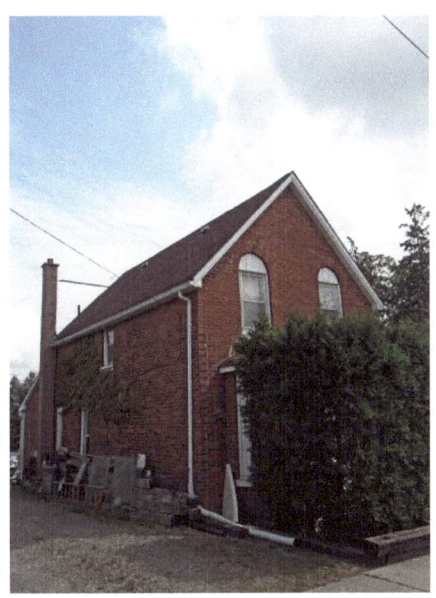

Main Street North - Gothic

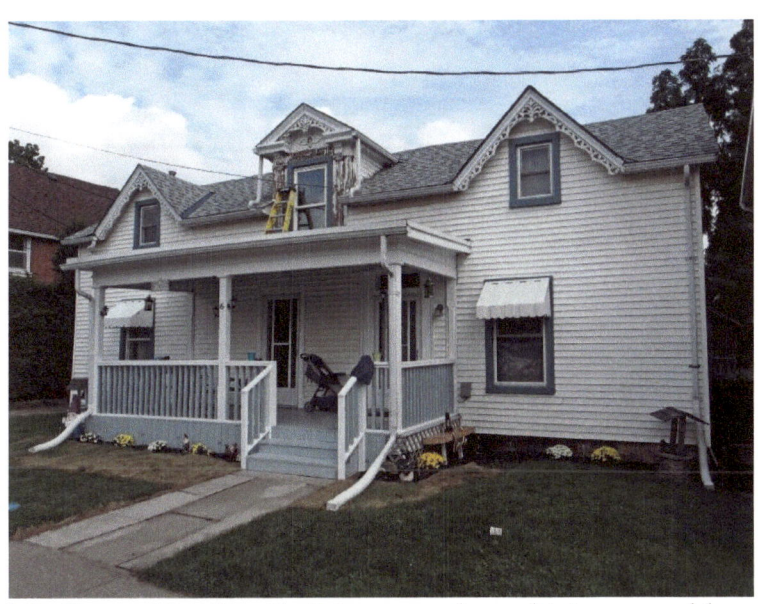

6 Main Street North – Gothic, verge board trim on gables and dormer

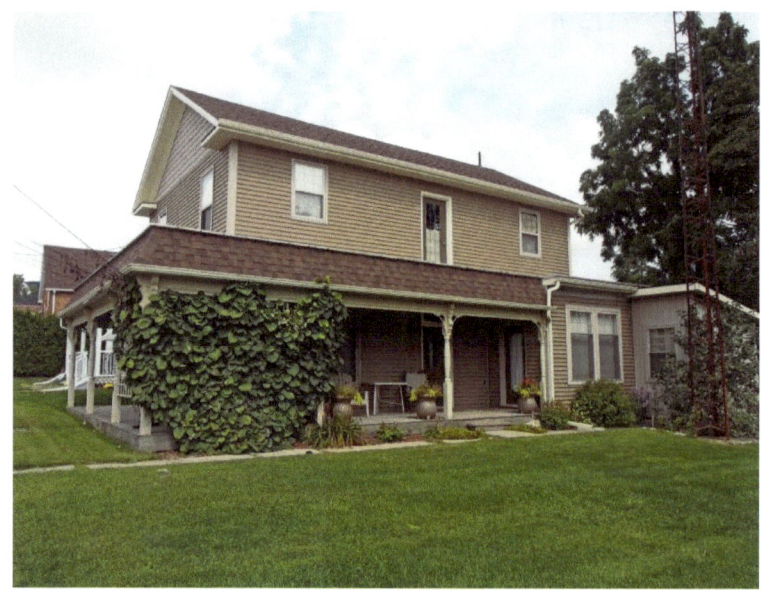

4 Main Street North – cornice return on end gable

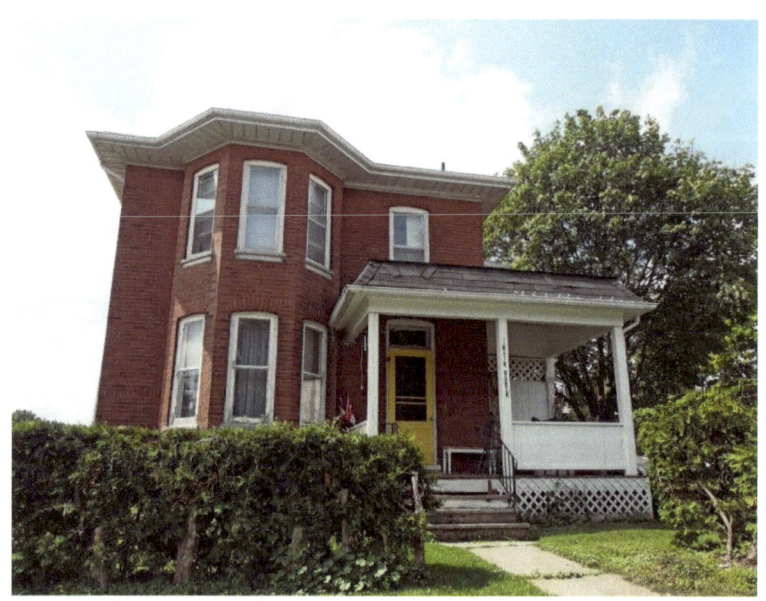

1 Main Street North – two-storey bay window, transom window above door

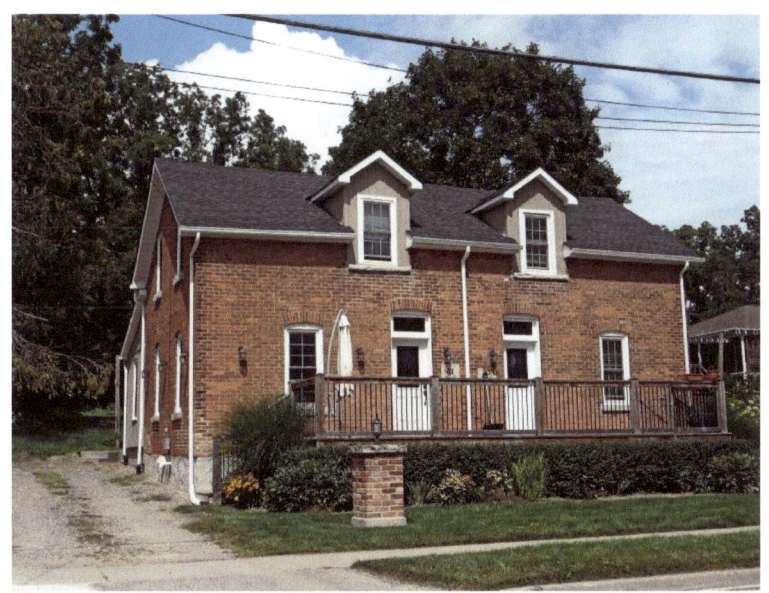
41 High Street – dormers in attic

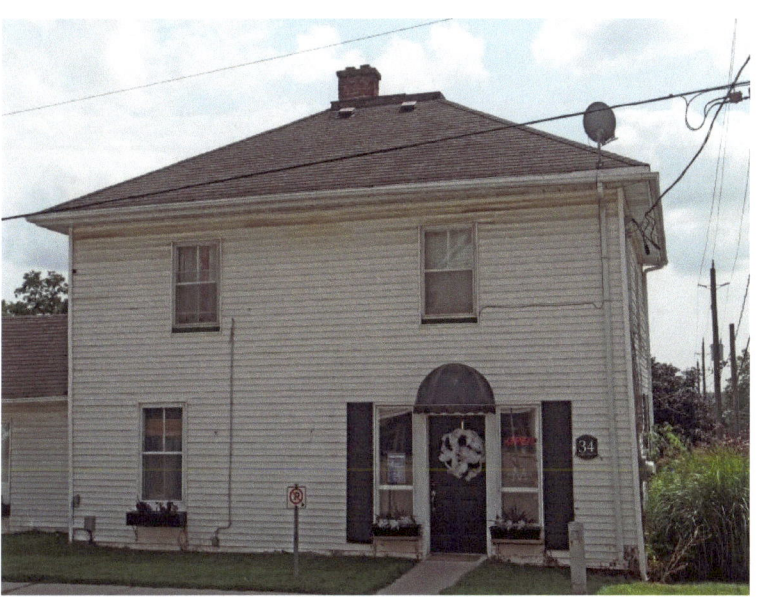
34 High Street

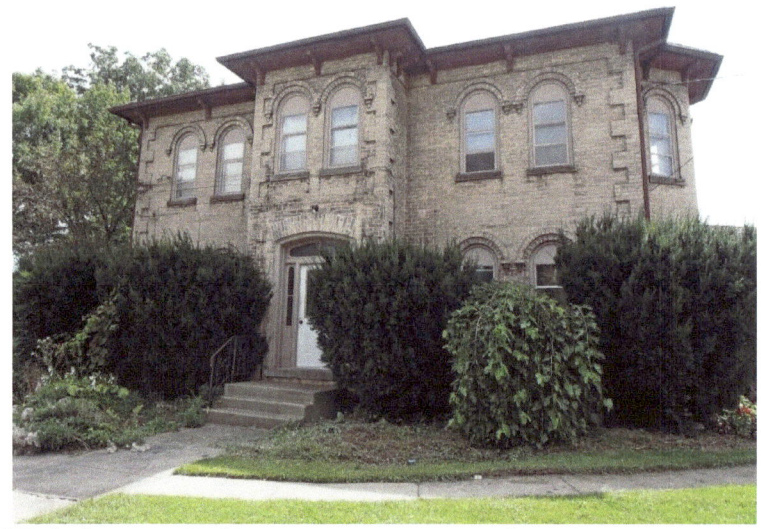

High Street – Italianate – two-storey frontispiece, corner quoins, cornice brackets, voussoirs

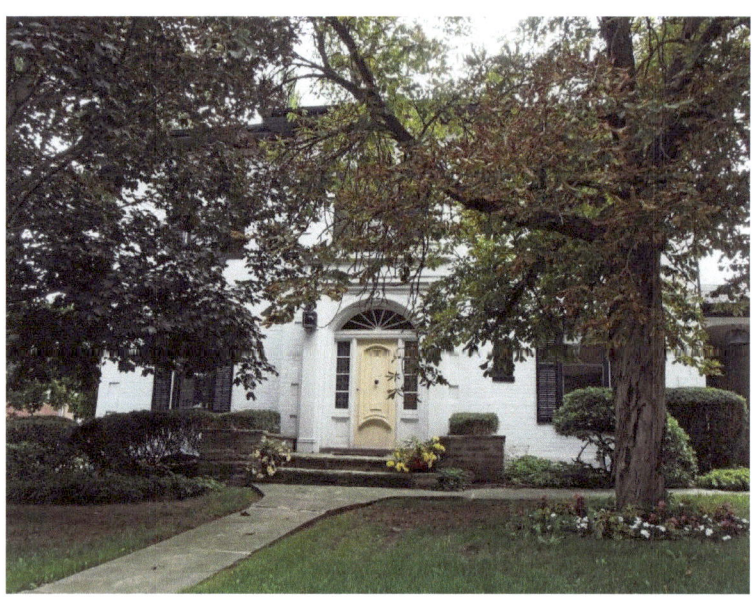

22 High Street – sidelights and transom window

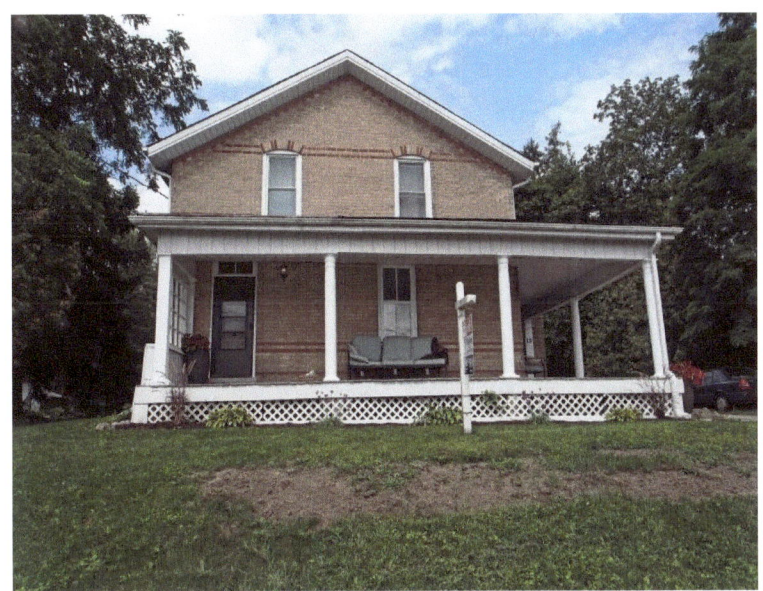

15 High Street – Gothic, dichromatic brickwork

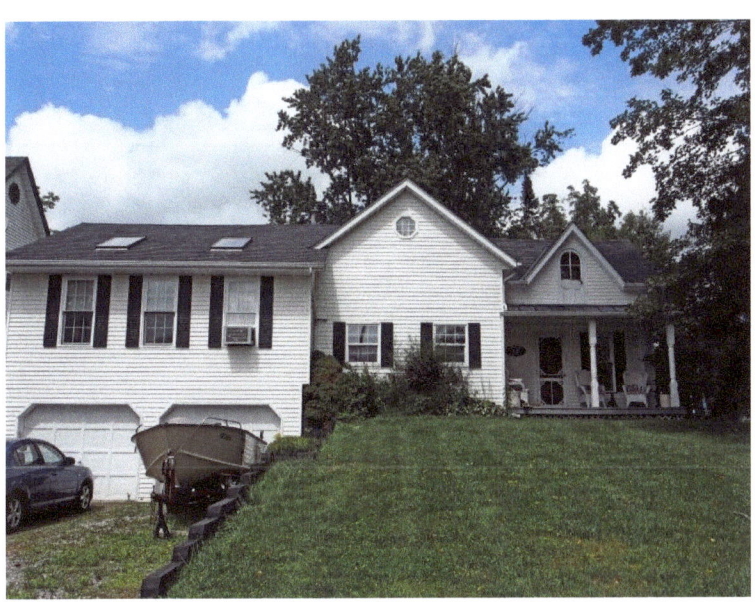

13 High Street

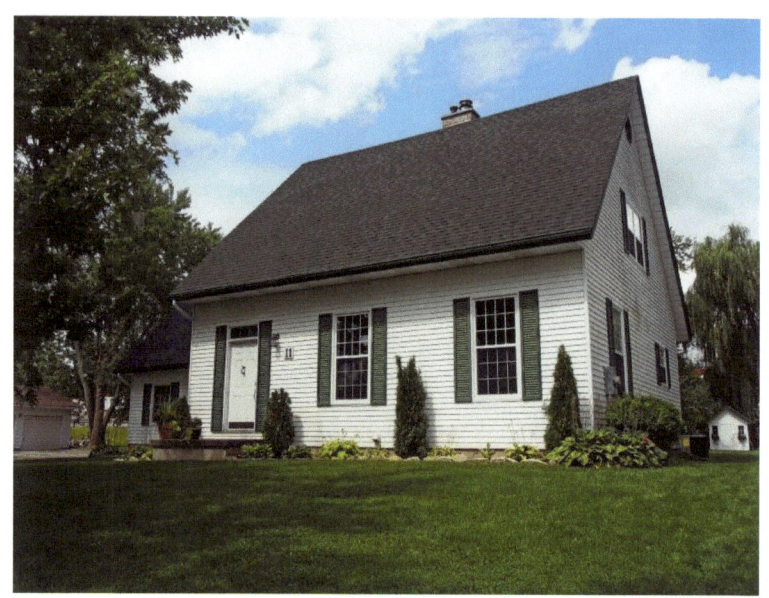
11 High Street

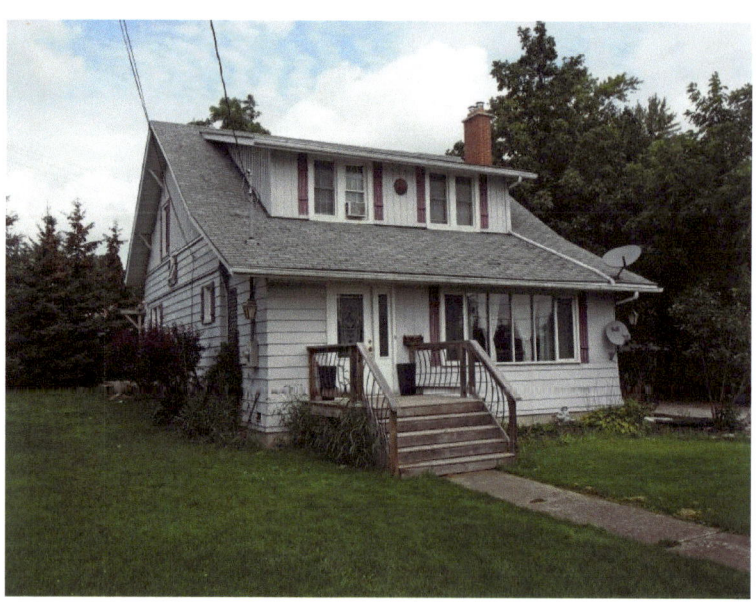
5 High Street – shed dormer

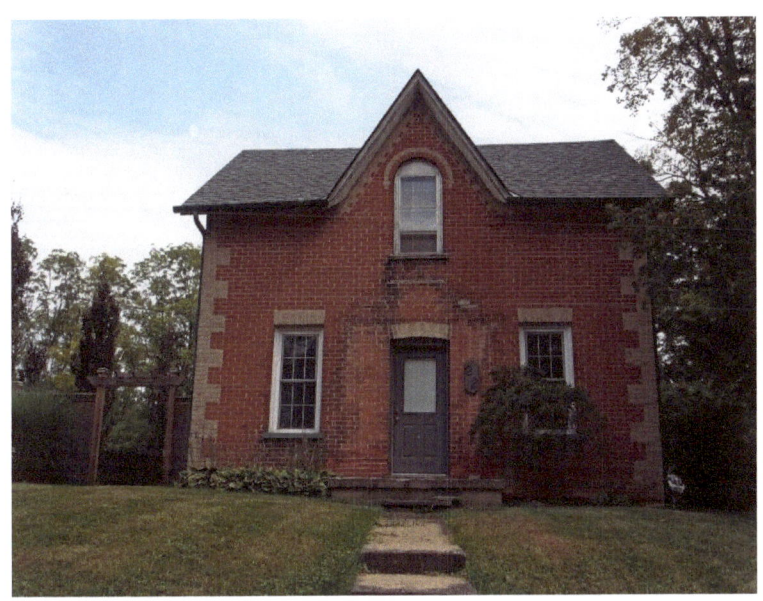

22 Tolhurst Avenue – Gothic, corner quoins

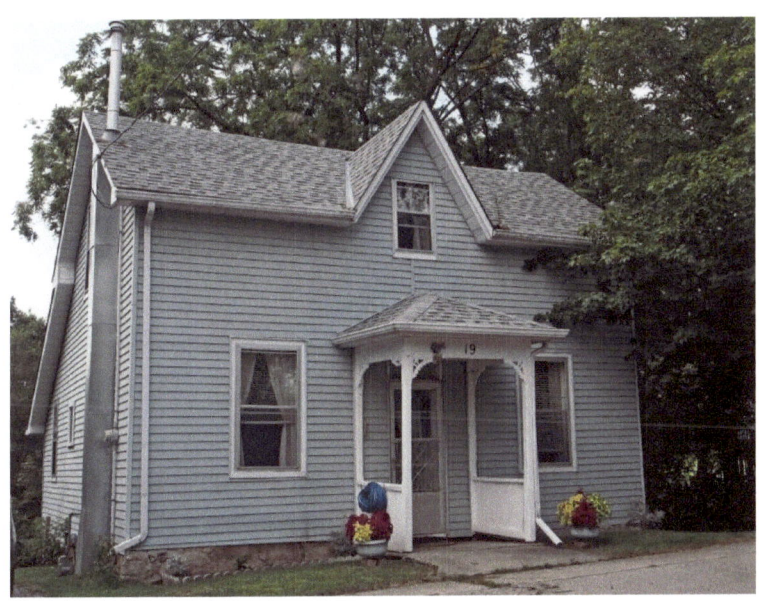

19 Tolhurst Avenue - Gothic

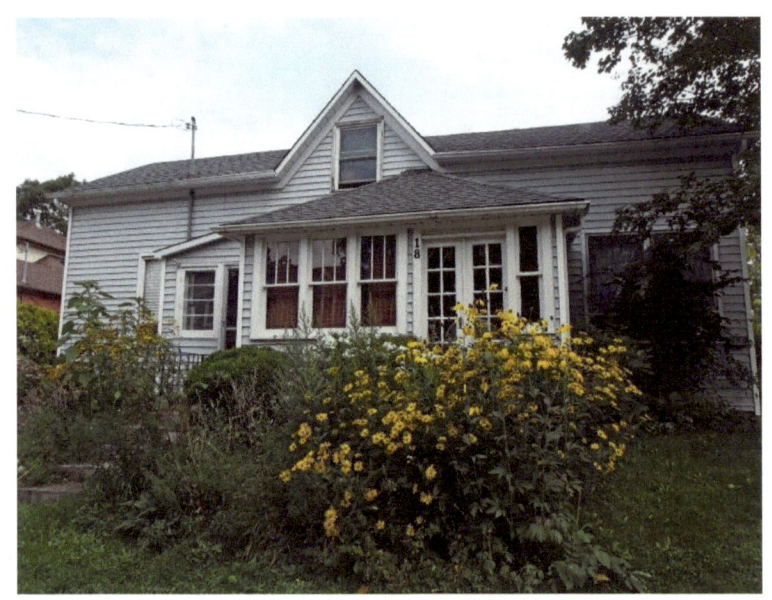

18 Tolhurst Avenue

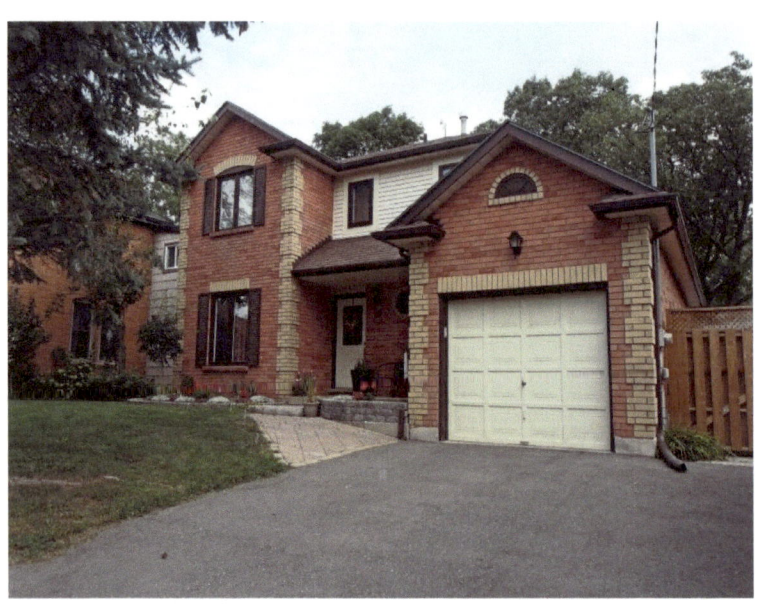

16 Tolhurst Avenue – corner quoins

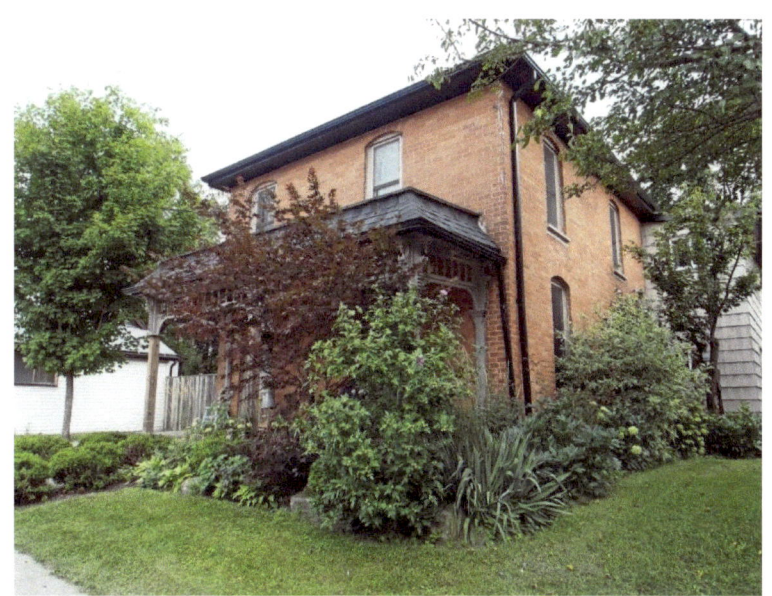

14 Tolhurst Avenue

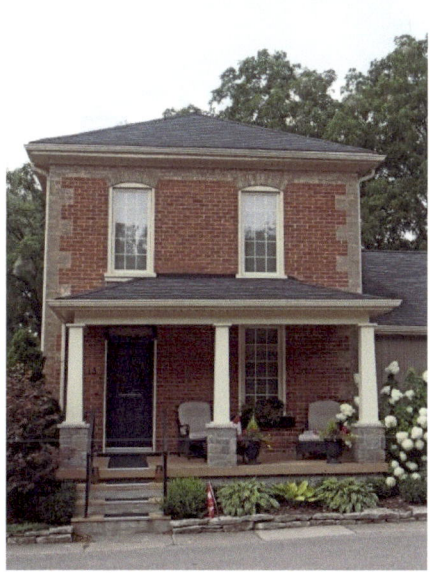

13 Tolhurst Avenue – voussoirs, corner quoins

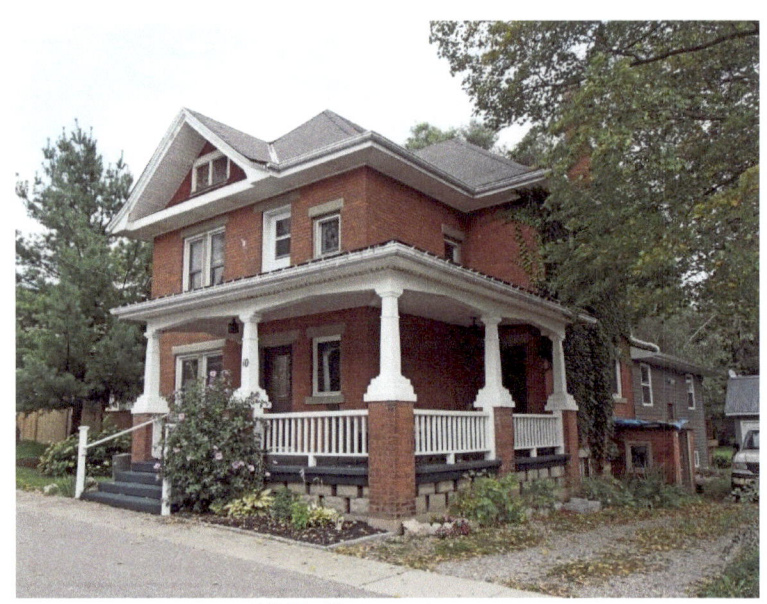

10 Tolhurst Avenue

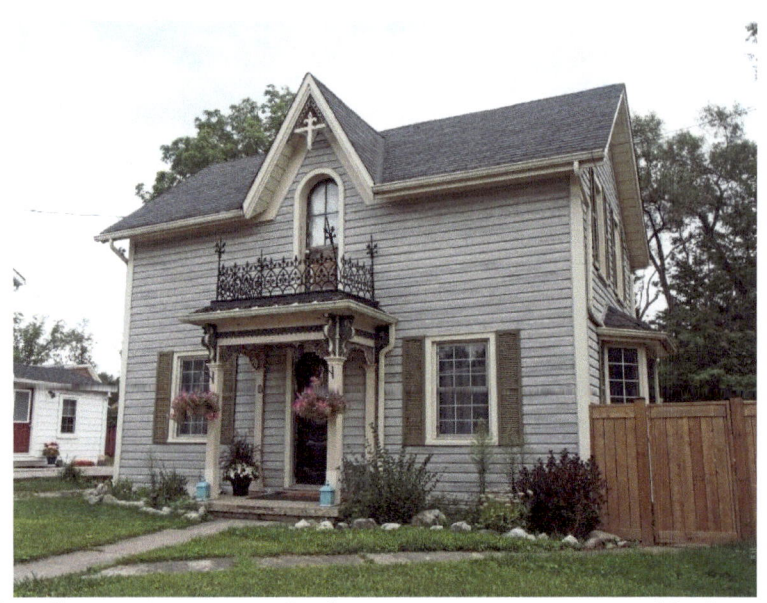

8 Tolhurst Avenue – Gothic, iron cresting around balcony

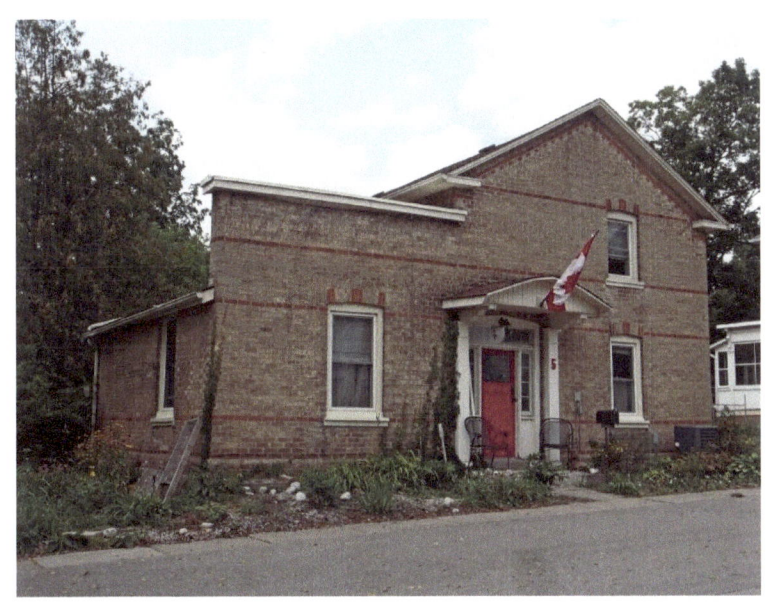

5 Tolhurst Avenue – dichromatic brickwork

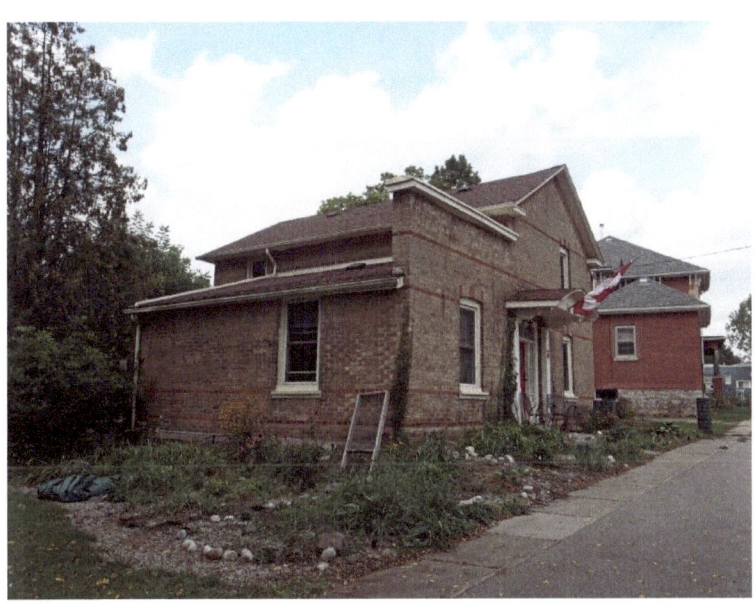

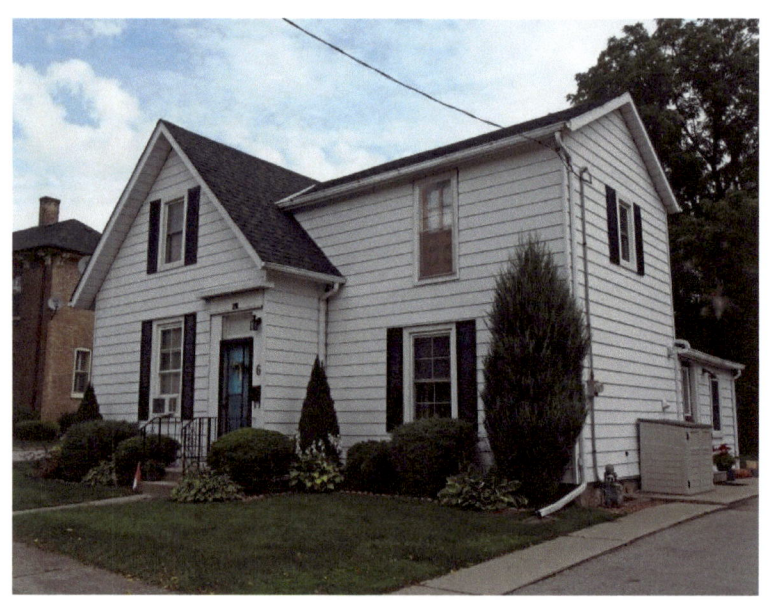
6 Tolhurst Avenue

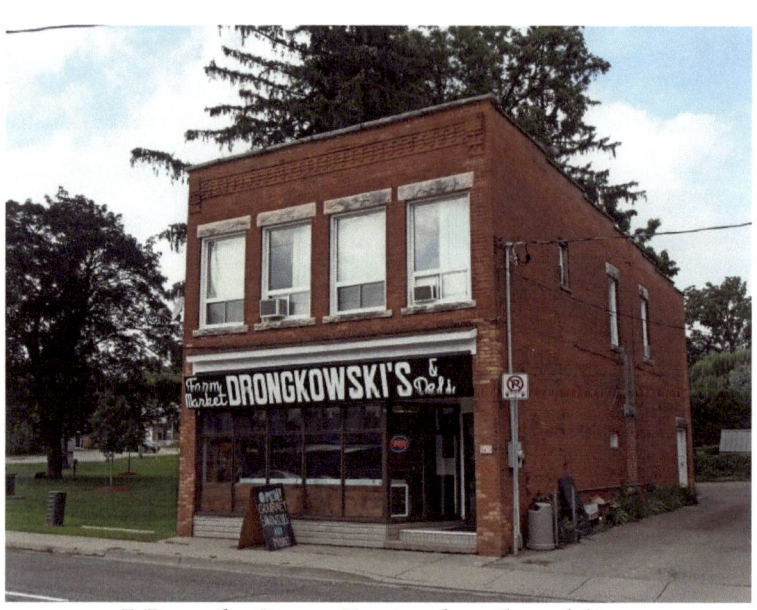
5 Beverly Street East – dentil molding

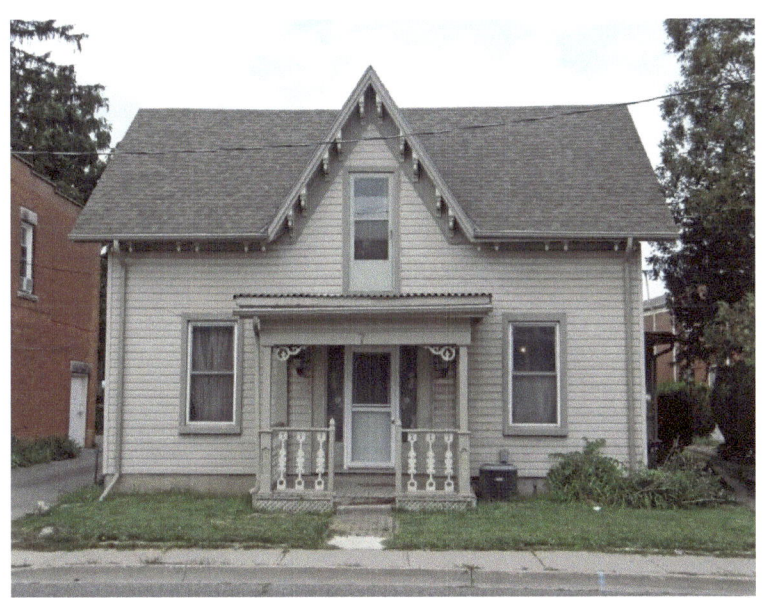

7 Beverly Street East – Regency Cottage, cornice brackets

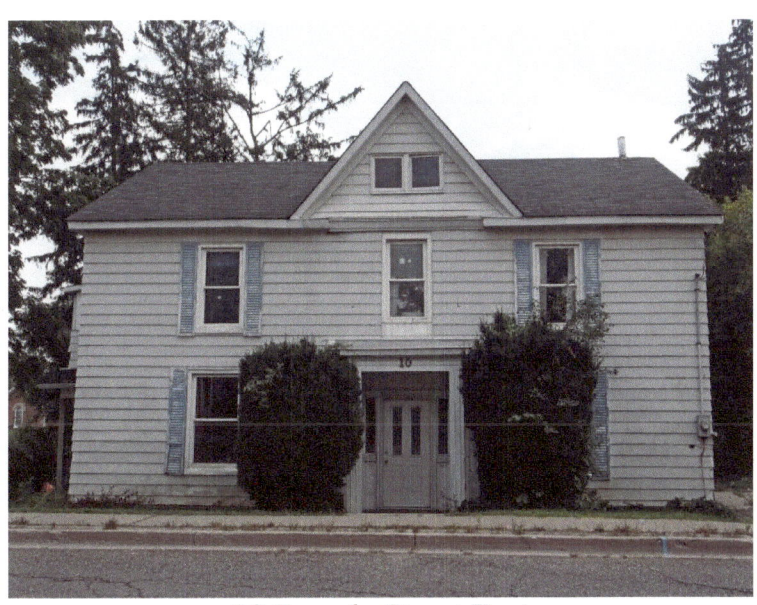

10 Beverly Street East

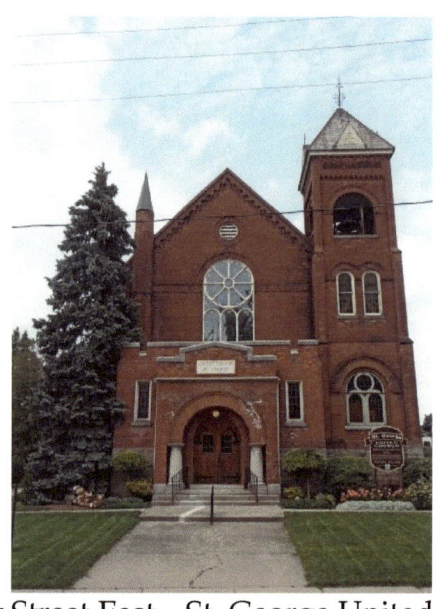

9 Beverly Street East – St. George United Church – Romanesque - rose window, three-storey bell tower, finials, buttresses

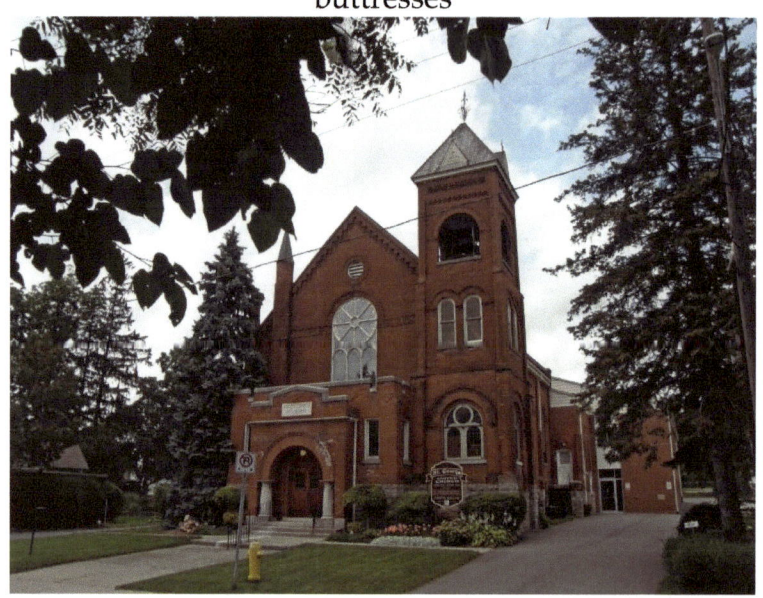

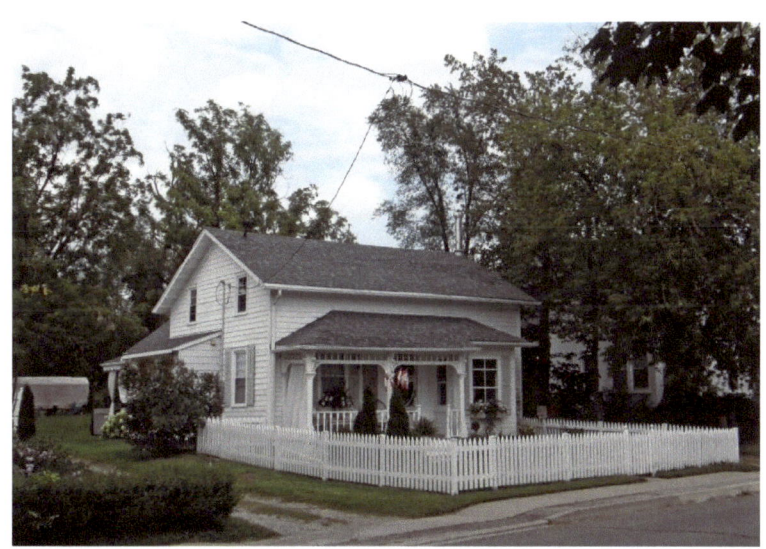

15 Beverly Street East

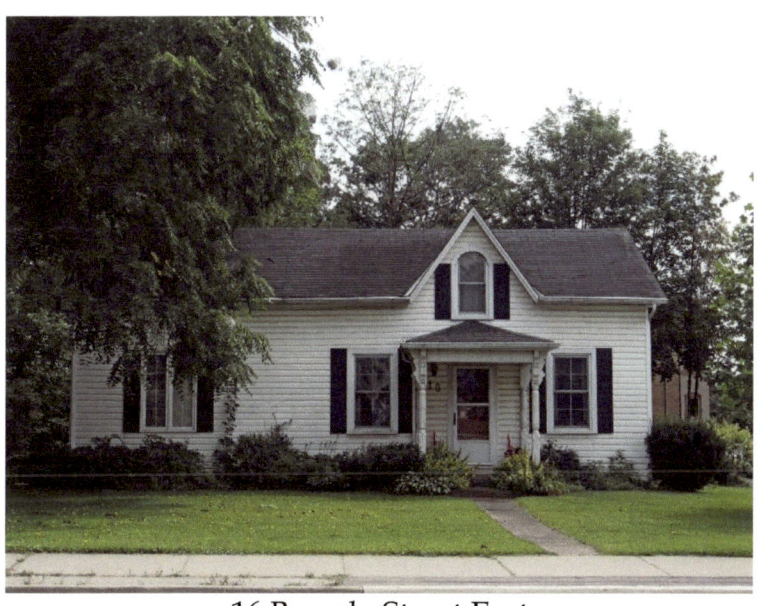

16 Beverly Street East

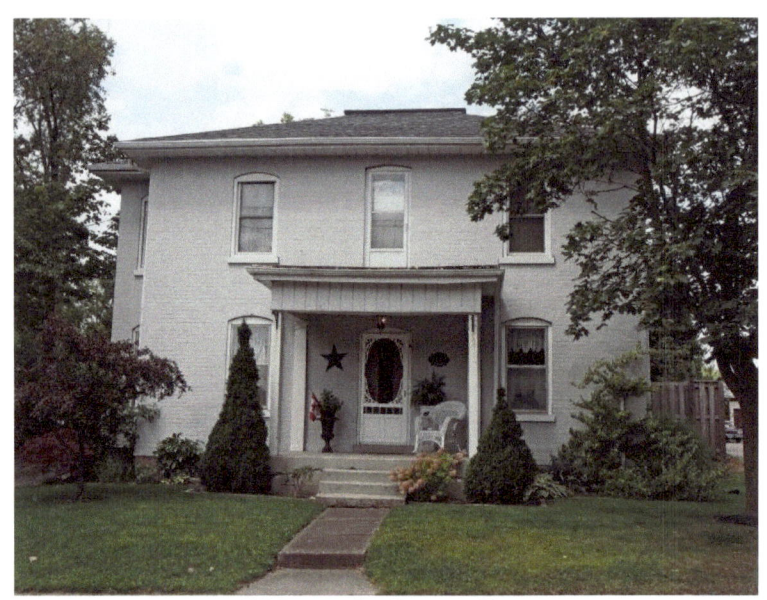

17 Beverly Street East

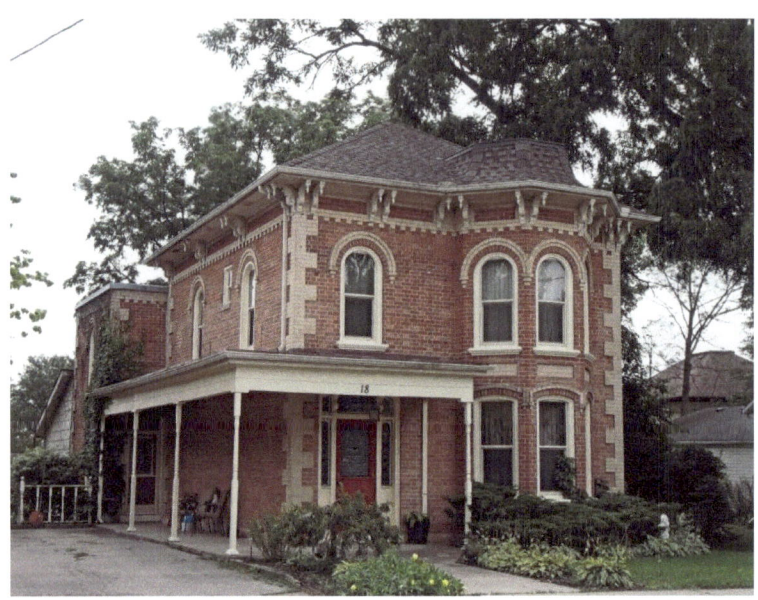

18 Beverly Street East – Italianate – paired cornice brackets, dentil molding, corner quoins, dichromatic brickwork

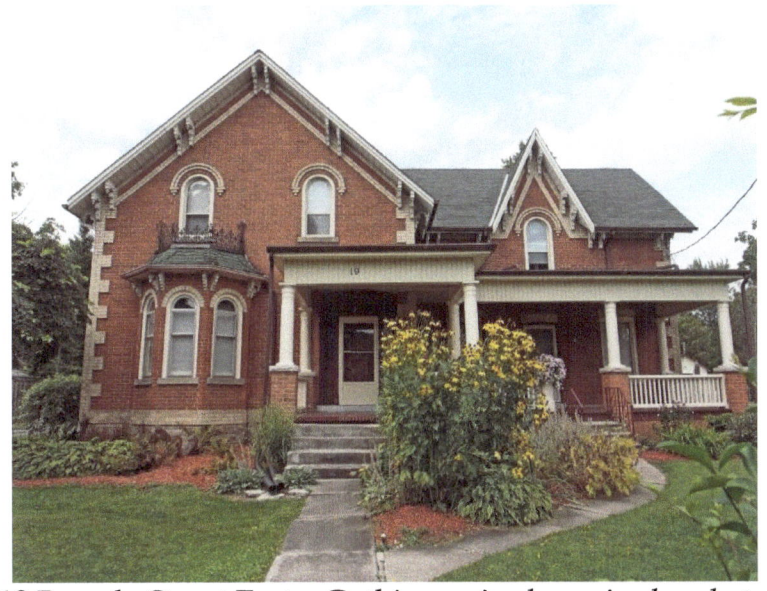

19 Beverly Street East – Gothic – paired cornice brackets, corner quoins, bay window

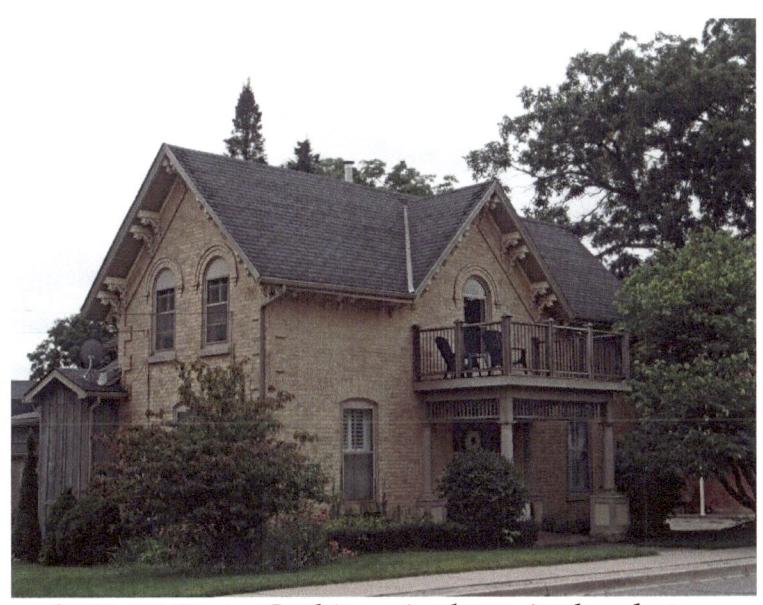

Beverly Street East – Gothic, paired cornice brackets, corner quoins, second floor balcony

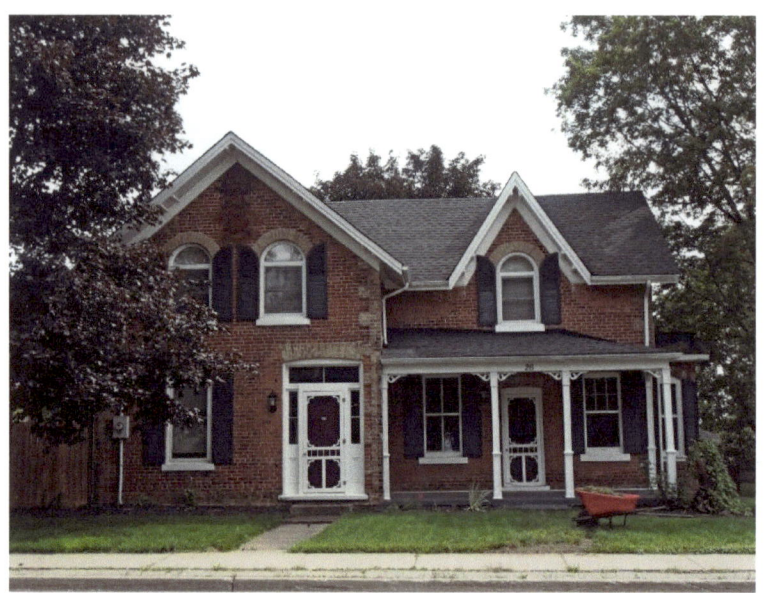

26 Beverly Street East – Gothic Revival, corner quoins

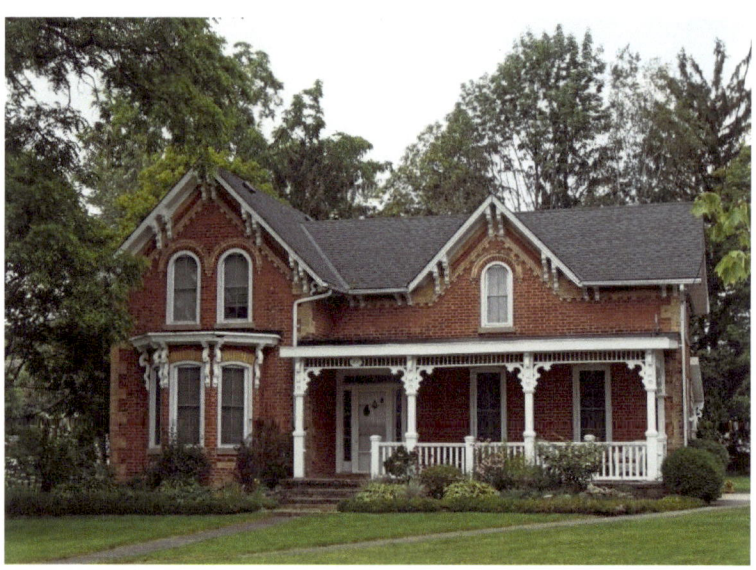

27 Beverly Street East – Gothic Revival, paired cornice brackets, dichromatic brickwork, bay window, bric-a-brac on verandah posts

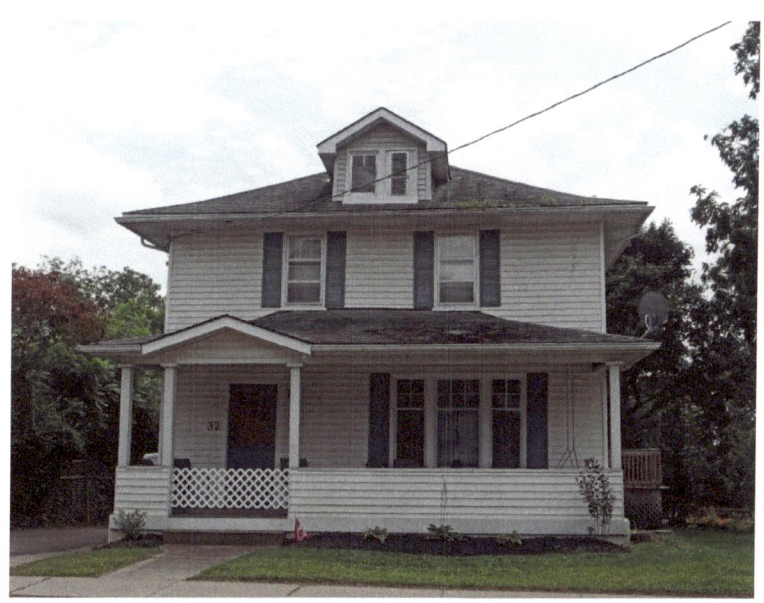
32 Beverly Street East – dormer in attic

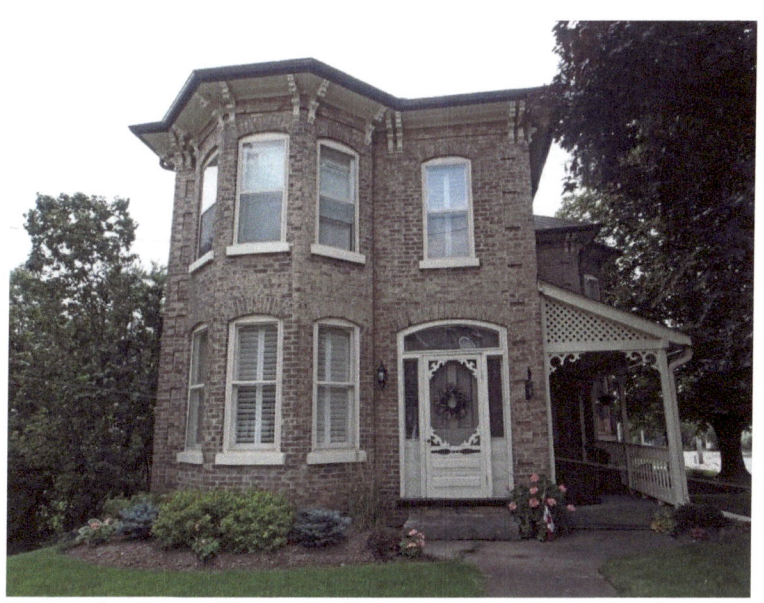
38 Beverly Street East – Italianate, paired cornice brackets, corner quoins, two-storey bay window

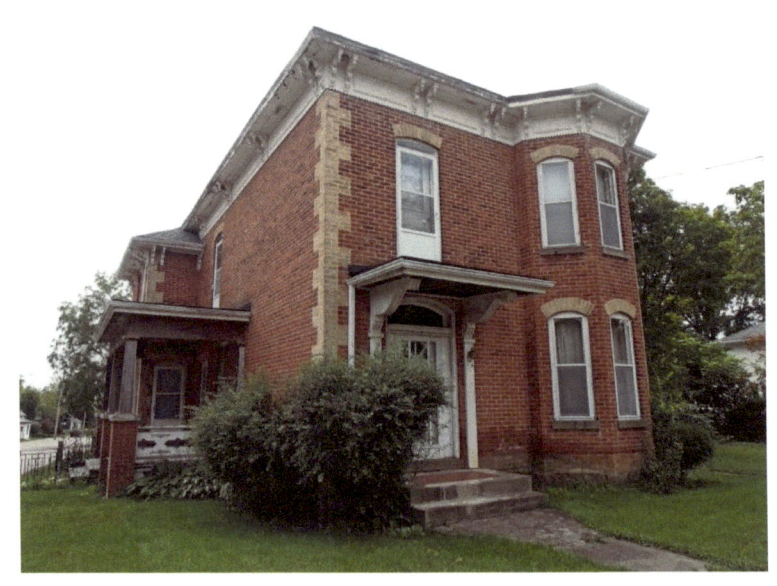

Beverly Street East – corner quoins, paired cornice brackets, two-storey bay window

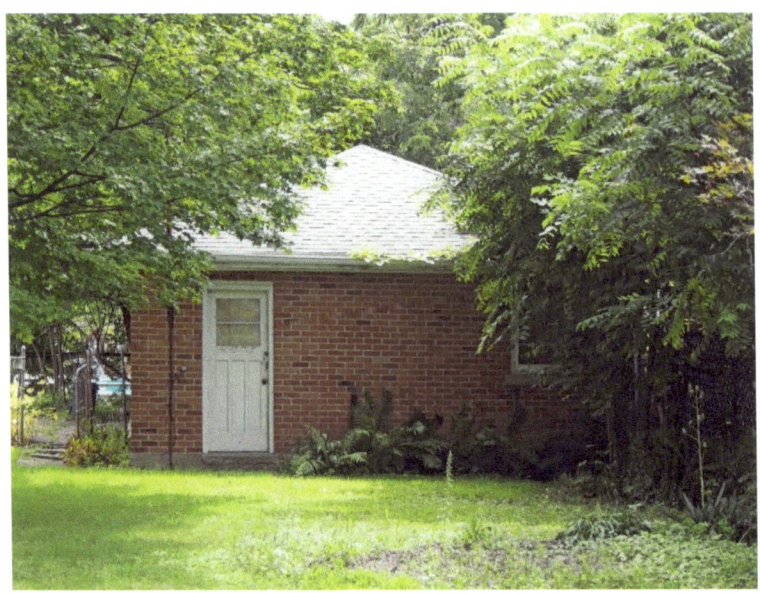

Shed on property

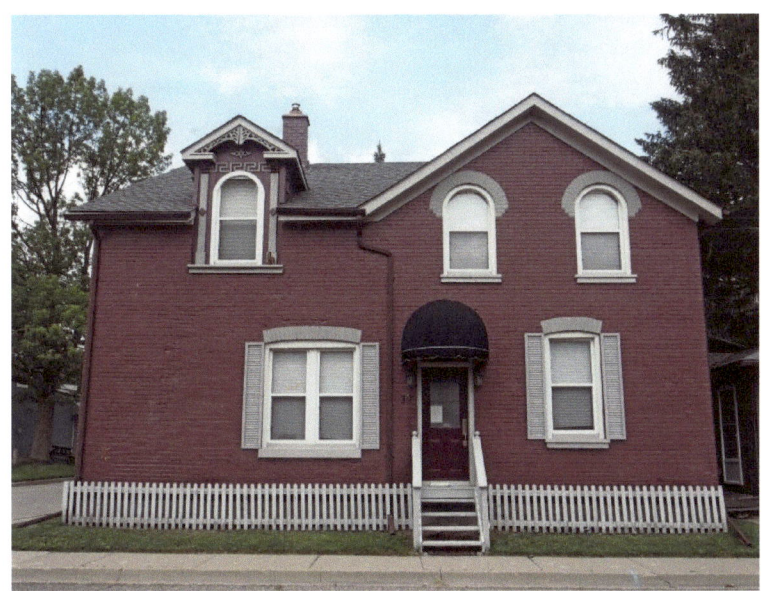

39 Beverly Street East – dormer with verge board trim and cornice return

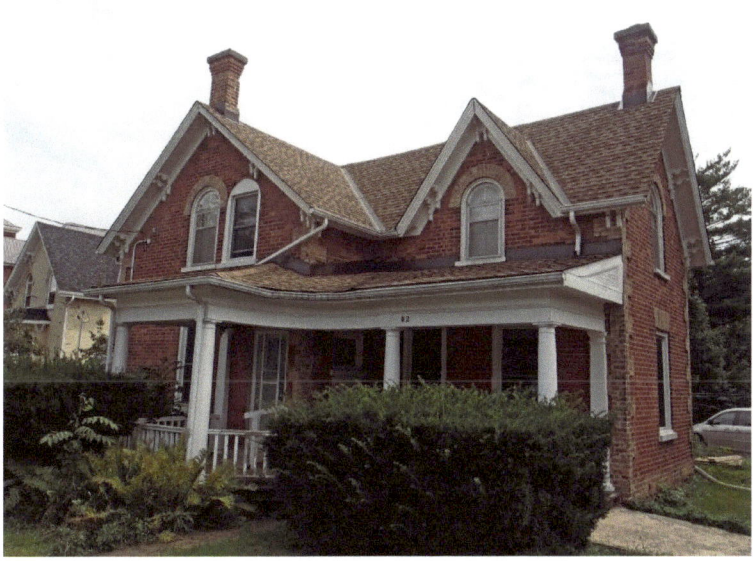

Beverly Street East – Gothic Revival – paired cornice brackets

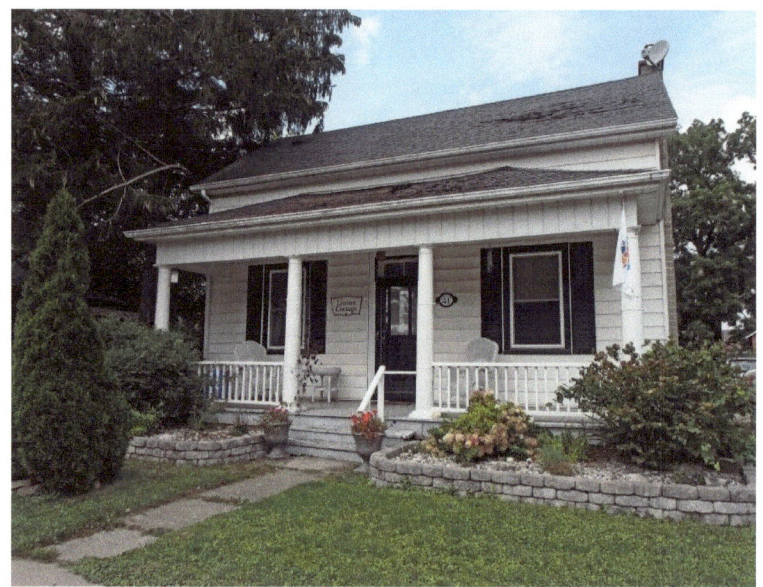

41 Beverly Street East – Linton Cottage c. 1890

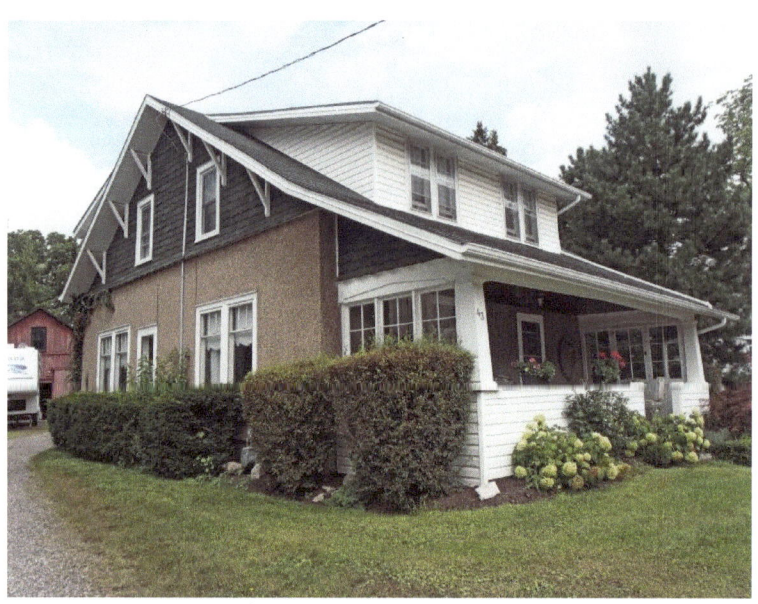

43 Beverly Street East – shed dormer

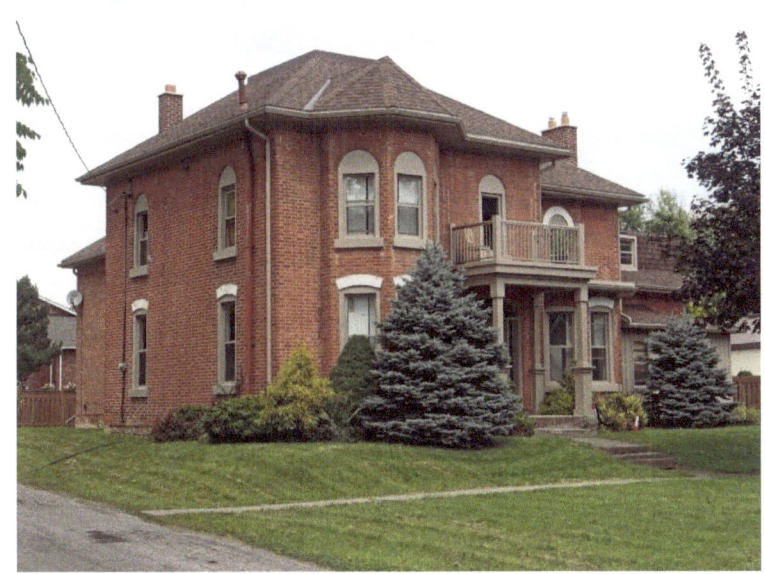

Beverly Street East – hipped roof, two-storey bay window

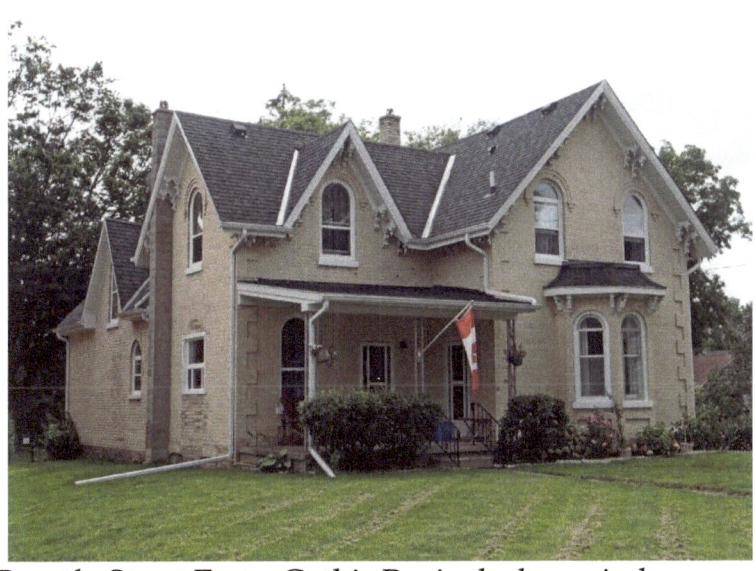

46 Beverly Street East – Gothic Revival – bay window, cornice brackets

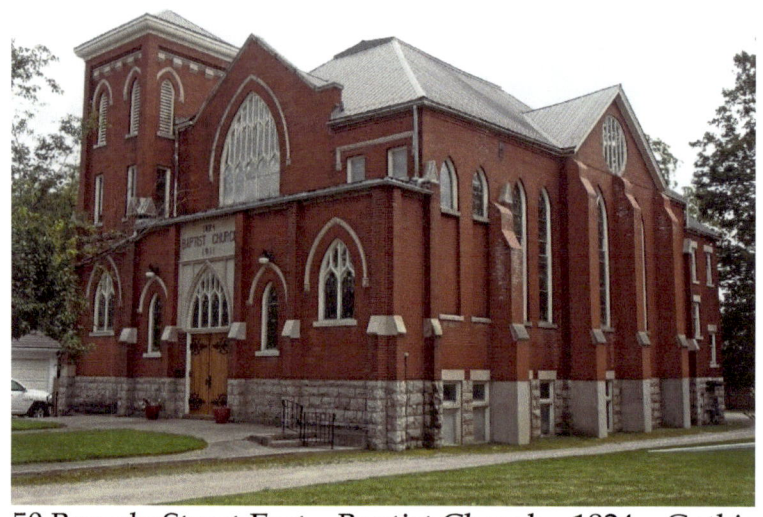

50 Beverly Street East – Baptist Church - 1824 – Gothic Revival, lancet windows, buttresses, muntins on some windows, three-storey tower

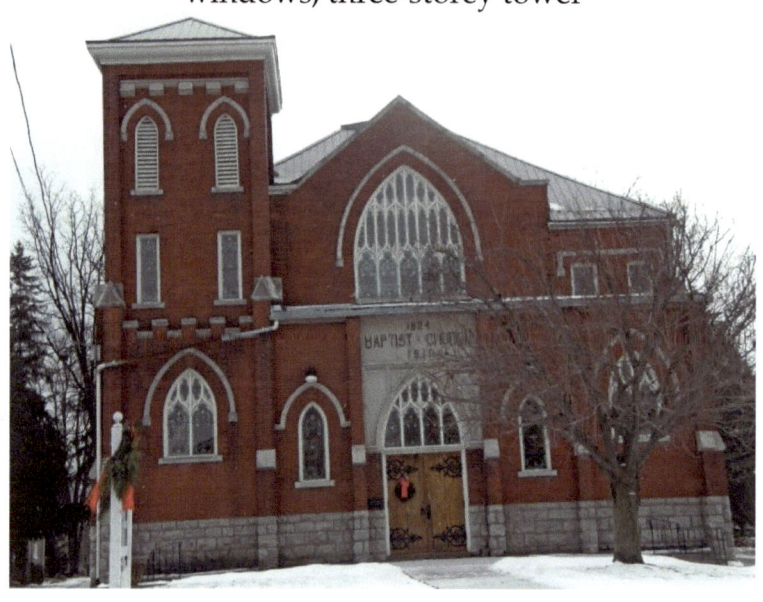

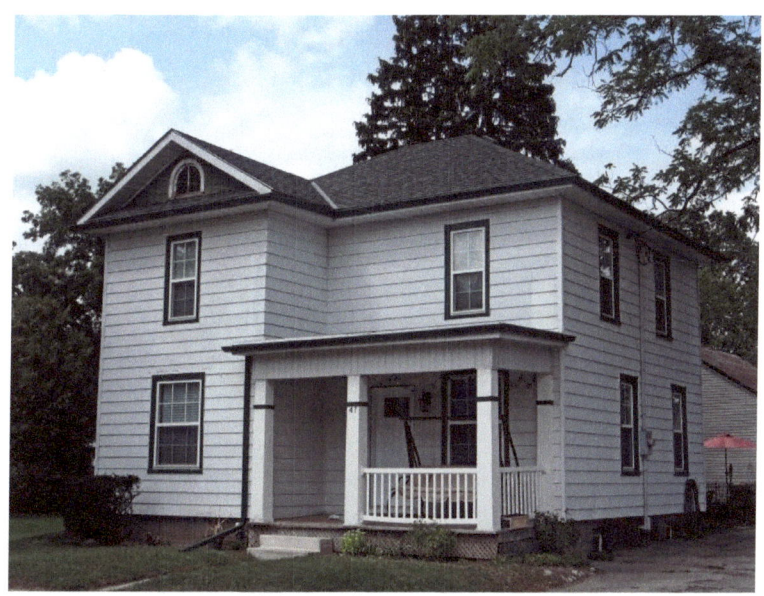

47 Beverly Street East

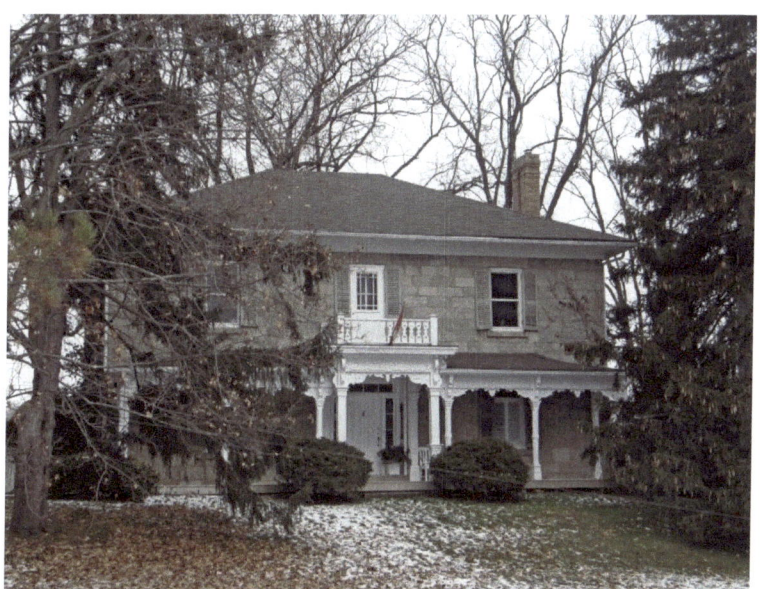

Nixon Homestead - 1853 - The Honourable Harry C. Nixon, Ontario's thirteenth premier was born on this farm. In 1913 he graduated from the Ontario Agricultural College. Nixon served in parliament for forty-two years.

Charles Nixon was born on the Niagara peninsula to a family of United Empire loyalists who had migrated to Canada after the American Revolution. As he was not the oldest son and would not inherit his parents' farm, once he was married he was furnished with a cart, oxen and other necessities and came to the County of Brant to homestead. Despite his young age he had learned the wheelwright trade. He built a house with his wife and had three children. Tragically, a plague swept the area and his wife and children died within two months of each other. By this time, his father had also died and left him with a significant inheritance. Charles took this inheritance and used it to purchase land in South Dumfries as well as to construct the stone house that stands there today. There he married again.

Harry Corwin Nixon began his Parliamentary career at the age of 28. He was elected the member for Brant in 1919 and continued in that capacity until his death in 1961. He became the provincial Secretary in the U.F.O. Labor government formed at the time by the Honorable E.C. Drury. Under the administration of Honorable Mitchell Hepburn, he became Premier of Ontario, taking the office on May 18 and resigning three months later after the government's defeat at the polls on August 17. He attended school in St. George, Brantford, and later the Ontario Agricultural College at Guelph where he received his B.S.A. degree. He married Alice Jackson of Lambton County.

Robert Nixon was born in St. George where he attended Public and Continuation Schools. He graduated from McMaster University in Hamilton in 1950 after studying the sciences and attended the Ontario College of Education in Toronto. In 1951 he went to teach in Sault Ste. Marie as a High School Biology teacher. In 1952 he married Dorothy Loveless of St. George and had two sons and daughters. He moved to Toronto to teach there in 1953, and then returned to St. George in 1954 to manage his father's farm. He taught at Pauline Johnson Collegiate and North park Collegiate before entering politics following the death of his father. There he became the provincial party head in 1967.

The homestead is a two storey single-detached building with a dual stack chimney linked at the top and located on the right side. The exterior walls are coursed cut stone with a rock-face finish and the house has a low gable roof. The upper level windows are two sash double hung while the lower level windows are two sash casement. There is a small balcony above the center two-panel door on the main façade.

Architectural Terms

Banding: Different materials, colors or textures used in horizontal bands along a wall. Example: 2 Main Street South, Page 25	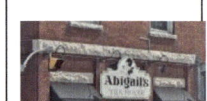
Bay Window: A window that projects out from a wall, in a semicircular, rectangular, or polygonal design. Used frequently in Gothic and Victorian designs. Example: 38 Beverly Street East, Page 53	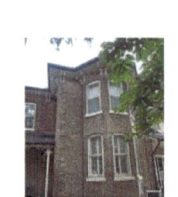
Brackets: a decorative or weight-bearing structural element which forms a right angle with one side against a wall and the other under a projecting surface such as an eave or roof. Example: 38 Beverly Street East, Page 53	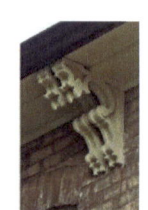
Buttress: a masonry structure built against or projecting from a wall which serves to support or reinforce the wall. In Canadian architecture, they are sometimes used for decoration. Example: 50 Beverly Street East, Page 58	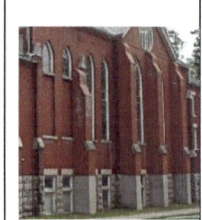
Cornice Return: decorative element on the end of a gable. Example: 5 Thompson Street, Page 6	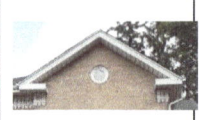

Cupola: A domed or curved roof rising from a building as a decorative element. Example: 39 Beverly Street West, Page 16	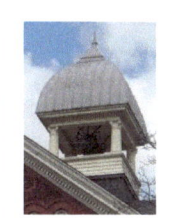
Dentil Moulding: an even series of rectangles used as ornamental decoration in cornices. Example: 39 Beverly Street West, Page 16	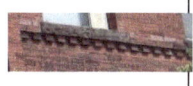
Dichromatic brickwork: the use of two colours of brick, tile or slate to decorate a façade. Example: 18 Beverly Street East, Page 48	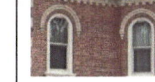
Dormer: (French for "sleep") a gable end window that pierces through the plane of a sloping roof surface to create usable space in the top floor or attic of a building by adding headroom. Example: 56 Beverly Street West, Page 14	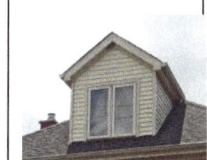
Entrance: The entrance encompasses the doorway and the inner vestibule or, in residential architecture, the covered porch. Example: 9 Beverley Street East, Page 48	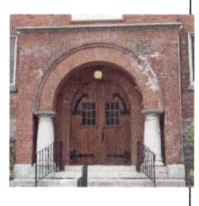
Gable: the triangular portion of a wall between the edges of a sloping roof. Example: 19 Beverly Street East, Page 51	

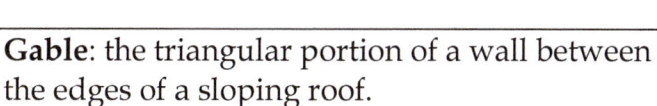

Hipped Roof: a roof where all sides slope downwards to the walls with no gables. Example: 54 Beverly Street West, Page 15	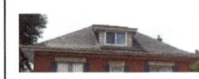
Iron Cresting: A decorative ornament along the top of a roof. Iron cresting was popular in the Baroque era and also in Italianate, Victorian, Second Empire and Queen Anne styles of architecture. Example: 8 Tolhurst Avenue, Page 44	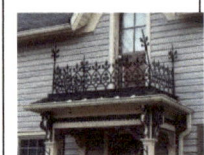
Keystones and Voussoirs: a voussoir is a wedge-shaped element used in building an arch. A keystone is the central stone that locks all the stones into position, allowing the arch to bear weight. A keystone is often enlarged and embellished. Example: 34-36 Main Street South, Page 21	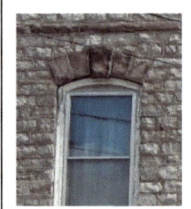
Lancet Window: a tall, narrow window with a pointed arch at its top. Example: 50 Beverly Street East, Page 58	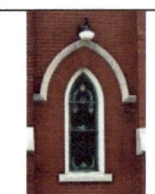
Muntin: When a window unit has more than one pane, the material that separates the panes is called the muntin. The larger, more decorative separations are called mullions. In stained glass windows, each piece of colored glass is held in place by a muntin. These were traditionally made of iron. Example: 50 Beverly Street East, Page 58	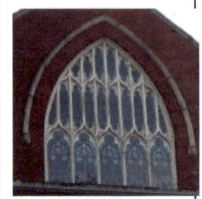

Palladian Window: a large window that is divided into three sections with the centre section larger than the two side sections and usually arched. Example: 29 Main Street North, Page 31	
Pediment: a triangular section above the door or portico, usually supported by columns. The inside of the triangle is called the tympanum. Example: 39 Beverly Street West, Page 16	
Porte-cochère: is a porch- or portico-like structure at a main or secondary entrance to a building through which a horse and carriage (or motor vehicle) can pass in order for the occupants to alight under cover, protected from the weather. In modern usage, portes-cochère are still used on some types of buildings such as major public buildings and hotels, where they provide pick-up and drop-off space. Example: 16 Main Street South, Page 25	
Quoin: masonry blocks at the corner of a wall, often a decorative feature, usually larger or of a different colour than the rest of the wall. Example: Beverly Street East, Page 54	
Rose Window: a circular window with ornamental tracery radiating from the centre. Example: 9 Beverly Street East, Page 48	

Sidelight: a vertical window that flanks a door, and is often used to emphasize the importance of a primary entrance. **Transom Window:** the light above the doorway, also called a fanlight. Example: 22 High Street, Page 38	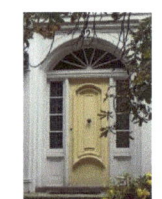
Tower: A circular, square, or octagonal vertical structure higher than the surrounding structure that is usually part of an existing building and is created either for extra defense or for a specific purpose such as a clock or a bell tower. Example: 9 Beverly Street East, Page 48	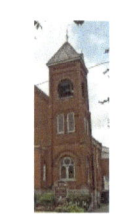
Terra Cotta (literally means "baked earth): was used as a decorative skin to cover or supplement brick and tiles of similar color in late Victorian buildings. The architect makes full-size drawings of all ornaments which are sent to the terra cotta manufacturer where a highly skilled modeler sculpts a clay model. The clay mixture is carefully hand-pressed into a plaster-of-Paris mold. Once the unit is dry, the mold is removed. After applying either a slip (clay and water) or a glaze, it is fired in a muffle kiln at a high temperature for several days. Example: 39 Beverly Street West, Page 16	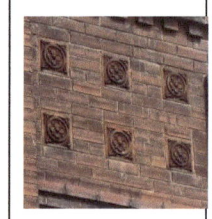
Verge board and Finial: also called bargeboards – hang from the projecting end of a roof and are often elaborately carved and ornamented. **Finial:** ornament added to the top of a gable, pinnacle, canopy or spire – a Gothic element. Example: 8 Tolhurst Avenue, Page 44	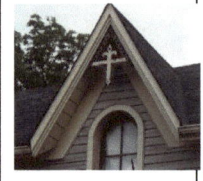

Building Styles

Georgian, before 1860 – This style began with the British King Georges in the 18th century. These buildings have balanced facades around a central door, medium-pitched gable roofs, and small paned windows. Example: 10 West Street, Page 9	
Gothic Revival, 1830-1890 – These decorative buildings have sharply-pitched gables with highly detailed verge boards, pointed-arch window openings, and dichromatic brickwork. It is a common style in Ontario. Example: 27 Beverly Street East, Page 52	
Italianate, 1850-1900 – A two story rectangular building with a mild hip roof, a projecting frontispiece, and generous eaves with ornate cornice brackets was the basis of the style; often there are large sash windows, quoins, ornate detailing on the windows, belvederes and wraparound verandahs. Italianate commercial buildings often have cast iron cresting and elegant window surrounds. Example: 6 Thompson Street, Page 6	
Ontario Cottage - one or one-and-a-half story buildings with a cottage or hip roof. The cottage roof is an equal hip roof where each hip extends to a point in the center of the roof. The hip roof has a long hip in the center. The Ontario Cottage is the vernacular design of the Regency Cottage which generally has a more ornate doorway and a partial or full verandah surrounding it. The roof can have a dormer, a belvedere, and generally two chimneys. Example: 30 Main Street North, Page 30	

Regency Cottage, 1830-1860 – This style originated in England in 1815 and spread to Ontario later in the 19th century as British officers retired to Canada. It is a modest one-storey house with a low-pitched hip roof and has a symmetrical front façade. Example: 7 Beverly Street East, Page 47	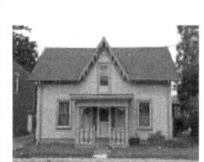
Romanesque Revival, 1880-1910 – This style hearkens back to medieval architecture of the 11th and 12th centuries with a heavy appearance, blocky towers and rounded arches. Example: 13 Main Street South, Page 27	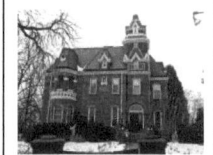

www.ingramcontent.com/pod-product-compliance
Lightning Source LLC
Chambersburg PA
CBHW040232220526
45473CB00001B/216